SWIPING FOR LOVE IN
ALL THE WRONG PLACES

TO Anca —

So grateful for
your support!
All the best!

♡ Karen
Cacioppo

SWIPING FOR LOVE IN ALL THE WRONG PLACES

KAREN HERRMANN

CACIOPPO

NEW DEGREE PRESS

SWIPING FOR LOVE IN ALL THE WRONG PLACES

ISBN   979-8-88504-099-0   *Paperback*

        979-8-88504-732-6   *Kindle Ebook*

        979-8-88504-211-6   *Ebook*

I dedicate this book to my amazing parents,
Dennis and Carol Herrmann!
I love you!

I dedicate it to all the people who believed in me, supported
me, and encouraged me throughout my book journey!

I also dedicate it to all of the people who are
discouraged with dating but keep putting themselves
out there to find their true "swipe-right"!

CONTENTS

PART 1:

ABOUT ME

CHAPTER 1

INTRODUCTION

—

Where do I begin to tell you about my crazy dating stories? When I first set off into my dating adventures, I had no clue I would still be "single" and writing this book more than ten years later, but I am. My inspiration and courage to write a book came from my inner strength to make a positive from a negative situation. I was very discouraged and had to find humor in my experiences while looking for love.

Dating was a terrifying notion to me back then, and I struggled to grasp the whole "dating" concept. I had just come out of a nine-year relationship with a person who was mentally and emotionally abusive. My friends urged me to get out of that relationship, but time and time again, I enabled the abuse. Then came the day when I had enough courage to walk away, and I brought that toxic chapter of my life to a screaming halt. That "*batshit crazy*" story is for another day and potentially another book.

The last time I dated was in college, and I met my now ex-husband in 1988, shortly after graduating from college. He was it for the next thirteen years, and then came my never-ending saga with the "nine-year guy." Dating was unchartered territory twenty years later.

"Nine-year guy" created some serious trust issues for me, and I was leery to move forward and find love.

I spent a year working on myself and healing the parts of me damaged from the emotional and mental abuse I endured.

My heart needed to heal, and it was imperative I loved myself before dipping my toe in the dating pond. I had only found true love twice before with my ex-husband and "nine-year guy." The thought of putting myself out there to date and possibly finding love again scared the hell out of me!

My single girlfriends had tried one or more of the many dating platforms. Some had success and ended up in a relationship or married, while others found themselves in their own brand of dating hell. Maybe I would be one of the lucky ones who would find their soulmate, fall in love, and live happily ever after. Little did I know how this would play out over the next decade!

I decided to bite the bullet and throw my hat in the dating arena.

I perused all of the dating sites and tried to determine which one was best suited for me. Do I pay for a dating service or just go on the free sites? I knew I shouldn't make such a decision so lightly. I based my decision on user reviews and went with the paid site. The only real benefit of the paid version was getting more qualified matches based on specific criteria. I figured, why not, so I paid for a three-month membership to one of the popular sites.

I heard many promising stories and hoped I would find my soulmate like so many others. I completed all the required fields and answered all the obligatory questions to complete my profile. I attached several favorite pictures of myself to complement my profile. I was nervous as my finger hovered over the "submit" button and click. In a split second,

I launched into my dating adventures. I officially entered into the black hole of dating.

I was very overwhelmed initially because I was considered "fresh meat" on the market to many of the habitual or serial daters. My profile attracted so many responses I didn't know what to do. This dating thing instantly became a full-time job, and I didn't anticipate that.

I hoped I wouldn't get carpel tunnel syndrome from all the "swiping left" I was doing. Holy crap!

I weeded out the men that were unmistakably not for me. I couldn't figure out how I matched with some of these yahoos and questioned this whole process! I was baffled by some of the ghastly profiles men created for themselves. The men I attracted ranged from utterly yummy ones to complete weirdos with no shirt, no teeth, long hair, and "coke bottle" glasses. I tried to keep an open mind, but it became more challenging as time went on.

I couldn't fathom what these guys thought when they created their profiles. Wouldn't they want their profile pictures to create the best first impression? I learned you only get one chance to make a first impression, so I was perplexed by all the fucked-up profiles people created to represent themselves.

Some profiles included only pictures of themselves wearing sunglasses or hats, which made me wonder if they were hiding something. How about the ones who didn't post a single picture of themselves but instead pictures of their motorcycles or pets? The ultimate pictures are the infamous topless bathroom selfies.

Some men considered it normal behavior to send unsolicited naked pictures of themselves, or of their privates, after knowing you for five minutes or less. I am not a prude by any means, but I expect a level of respect while getting to know someone. I was completely taken aback by this conduct.

I started texting with several gentlemen after riffling through all the minutia, which was a huge time investment, by the way. I found some conversations quite enjoyable, while others were flat-out offensive.

I learned throughout my dating trials and tribulations not to share my cell phone number or "digits" with someone too early in the dating process. I am not a big phone talker in general, but certainly not in the early stages of getting to know someone. Some guys want to talk for hours every night, and then you learn there is no connection when you meet. I made the mistake of sharing my information prematurely on several occasions and learned to regret it.

Some men mandated you talk to them on the phone, or they would not agree to meet you in person. I've declined meeting someone as a result of this demand because I don't do ultimatums. Some men base their whole connection with you on a simple phone call.

Personally, I need to meet someone in person to determine whether there is a connection or true attraction with someone worth pursuing. A guy may be eye-catching in his profile photos, but that doesn't necessarily translate to his personality. I usually know after the first date if there will be a second. I have tried to give guys the benefit of the doubt if the first date was a bust. If he truly seemed like he had potential, I gave him a second chance to shine.

I went in dating waves that lasted from two weeks to three months. Sometimes I would get incredibly frustrated by it all. I removed myself from dating all together. I would go on a *dating hiatus* that lasted anywhere from one month to one year. Something would inspire me to try dating again, and I would pull up my big girl panties and forge ahead into dating once again.

I hoped that one day I would find the guy who would be my "end chapter"! Finding that person would be a wonderful thing. I often get asked the million-dollar question, "How has a beautiful woman like you not been scooped up?" That question is very easy for me to answer, and some find my response difficult to grasp. I say, "I am an independent, self-sufficient woman who loves her amazing life. I don't have to account for my time, answer to anyone, and I can come and go as I please. A man won't complete me. He will enhance my life." The person who becomes my "end chapter" must be amazing.

One night I will always remember after being on the dating market several months, is when my best friend and I met at our usual location for the *half-priced bottle of wine night!* It had been quite a while since we caught up, and she had a lot of exciting things going on in her life. I dedicated the next forty-five minutes to hearing about the new man in her life. She had been there done that in the dating world, but this guy seemed special to her. She lit up when she told stories about him and talked about their future, which had never happened before. She was in love, and it showed!

Her story reestablished my faith in dating because I watched her move from relationship to relationship over the years. When she finished her life updates, she looked at me and asked, "How is the dating world treating you?"

I said, "Buckle your seatbelt!"

At the time I met with my girlfriend for happy hour, I had only been on eight dates. One by one, I told her about some of the dates I had been on. "Alligator Arms," "A Legacy in my Own Mind," "The Sore Loser," "Rotten Teeth Guy," "Boop Guy," and "The Fishhook Kisser," in addition to a few others.

Little did I know, this was only the tip of the iceberg of my dating adventures. My girlfriend laughed so hard she was crying! The man sitting next to us at the bar leaned over and said, "You are hilarious! I have been listening to your stories and am cracking up over here. I haven't laughed that hard in ages. You need to take that on the road and do stand-up comedy!" He questioned if those were true stories, and I said, "*I can't make this up!*"

I looked at her and said, "I am so discouraged by these weirdos I have met. Why can't I find a normal guy?" She smiled and said, "Don't give up! I found a good one, so they are out there! You just haven't met him yet." I had to keep on keeping on and have the faith I would find a good guy one day!

She looked at me at said, "*You should write a book!*"

I started journaling all of my dates going forward and those I had already had. Each date got a chapter name that represented the defining detail of that person.

Now let's get to the juicy stories that will blow your mind. Just know, no matter how weird or horrible you think your story is, I believe you! When people tell me their story and say, "You'll never believe this!" I can tell you I will. I know 100 percent you are telling me the truth. There isn't a story that is too strange, too crazy, too f'd up, or too mind-boggling to believe! This shit is real, and we can't make it up if we tried. If you have contemplated dipping your toe in the dating pond, you may not want to after reading these stories, but I am here to tell you that you need to keep on keeping on. Use my stories as a path or guide to what to watch out for, and just proceed with caution. We all make mistakes while dating. My friends have questioned me on many occasions about my decisions on dates. They would ask, "Why did you stay? I would have left in five minutes! I would have tossed my wine on him and left."

My stories will resonate with anyone brave enough to keep putting themselves out there in the cesspool of dating. It is like finding a diamond in a dumpster, but I keep trying, and I won't settle. You are not alone in your dating hell, and together we can turn your frustration into hilarity. I am reassured to know I am not alone in with my crazy ass stories, and the struggle bus of dating is real

I would be rich if I had five dollars for every time someone said, "I would buy that book." You are reading the introduction of my first book, which means that you bought a copy. I want to thank you for your support and contribution to my book journey!

CHAPTER 2

MY IDEAL GUY

———

"Are you dating anyone?" or "Do you have any good dating stories to share?" If I had a dollar for every time someone asked me one of those questions, I would be a millionaire and could retire tomorrow! Historically, my answer is one of two responses. The first is my token answer, "I'm doing the online dating thing, but it's a joke, and I can't find a normal guy if he landed on me naked." My fallback answer is, "Dating is frustrating, so I had to take a break from all these assholes, and I'm on a dating hiatus until further notice."

Some imply perhaps I am being too picky. Friends caution me who say there is no such thing as a picture-perfect man, and I'll end up alone if I wait for perfection. I refuse to settle for someone who doesn't check the boxes for me.

The person I spend the rest of my life with has to be "that guy" for me.

What is picky? Can we define it? My person doesn't have to have several residences in various parts of the country to accommodate each season as a prerequisite. He doesn't need an assortment of cars in the garage to match his mood. The qualities I look for in a person are pretty straightforward and not unrealistic. There are certain things I would tolerate and others I won't budge on. I am a self-sufficient, independent woman, and I am not ashamed of being single. A man needs to show me how he is going to enhance my life and make it better than it already is.

I ask myself, *"What does he bring to the table?"*

I look for a handful of "must-have" qualities in a life partner. He needs to fit the following criteria:

- A decent career with ambition to be successful, not just complacent
- A car that isn't a minivan, rust bucket, or twenty plus years old
- A house, meaning he doesn't live in his parent's basement
- Children that are old enough they don't require a babysitter (preferably older than eighteen)
- Must be a nonsmoker—a deal breaker for me
- Must have an outgoing personality to complement mine, no wallflowers
- He must be a good kisser
- I will not tolerate a deceptive or manipulative person
- I will not tolerate addictive habits
- Hypocrites are not welcome
- Control freaks need not apply

Let me elaborate on each of these so you get the big picture.

The guy must have a successful career. I don't care if he has a college degree or not, just as long as he has a lucrative and stable occupation. I have seen many men succeed in life without having a college education. Some women demand a man have a college degree, or they won't give him the time of day. I am not that person. It's about having life goals and succeeding at them. The bottom line is I am not going to support him, pay his bills, or be his sugar mama.

He must have a normal vehicle. What is normal? Normal is a car from this decade, which runs well, and isn't in the shop every other week. Preferably not a minivan! The vehicle should run well, have four wheels, is clean on the inside, isn't a rust bucket, doesn't have stained seats, and doesn't reek of smoke. I would never go on a date in someone's work vehicle like a van, a truck with T bars, or a food truck. On one occasion, my date picked me up in a car that looked like it came straight out of a junkyard, and I was so embarrassed. I wasn't sure the car would make it down the street, much less downtown. Another time, a date picked me up in an old rusty minivan from the 80s. This shitcan van needed a restart every time it came to a stop, and a couple of times, I thought it was dead. I couldn't wait for the date to end and never looked back.

I always get lots of chuckles when I talk about the next topic. My guy needs to live in a typical residence like an apartment, condo, or home and not in his parent's basement. I'm not heartless or unsympathetic should a parent's health or medical events warrant alternative living arrangements. If this "parent" scenario presented itself, I would need to contemplate the viability of that relationship going forward. I've heard of so many odd living situations over the years. Nothing surprises me. If you can't afford your own place, then you are not my guy, and that's the bottom line!

The condition of a man's residence can be very telling and speaks a thousand words. You can learn if someone is a neat freak, slob, hoarder, or somewhere in between just by seeing the setting of where he lives. Dating a person who doesn't want you to see his place is a giant *red flag*!

My children have ranged from teenagers to grown adults while I have been in the dating arena. A man having children is not a problem, as long as they don't require a babysitter. I want to have the freedom to be spontaneous at a moment's notice with my man, and our plans shouldn't be dependent on the availability of a babysitter. Some men expect you to participate in their children's extracurricular activities or be the fill-in parent when he is unavailable. I've been there, done that, and am not interested in repeating it!

What is a total deal breaker for me? A guy who smokes. I can't tell you how many men I've met that say they don't smoke when in fact, they do. If you are a nonsmoking person, it is very obvious when you meet someone who does. I don't want a guy who smokes pot on a regular basis. I don't mind the guy who enjoys an occasional cigar, as long as he brushes his teeth before kissing me. Kissing a smoker is like putting your tongue in an ashtray. Ick! If you are a cigarette smoker, you are not an option for me.

Let's talk about another nonnegotiable quality when it comes to my ideal guy. This topic is *not* open for discussion. My guy *must* have an outgoing personality and a great sense of humor. I am a very social, outgoing person with a large social circle. The *"wallflower"* type will not last long in my world. I dated people who hardly muttered a single word to anyone but me at a social function. My guy needs to be comfortable mingling around and making conversation with other people on his own. The last thing I want to do at a social function is babysit my date.

Having a good belly laugh with your person is a marvelous thing. My soulmate needs to have this quality because I love laughing and having fun. My guy needs to know how to do the same.

So many men just aren't good kissers, and it is a key element to intimacy. A great kisser has the ability to get you close to orgasm just from kissing. My guy must be sensual and know how to kiss with passion. I am shocked that so many men have missed this critical lesson in their lives and are horrible kissers. There are many names for these bad kissing techniques.

The toilet bowl kisser uses his tongue to swirl the inside of your mouth. The lip or tongue suckers insist on sucking your tongue or lip verses just kissing you. The fishhook kisser puts his finger in the corner of your mouth while he's kissing you. Who wants someone's finger your mouth while they're kissing you? Some guys are just sloppy, gross kissers and want to coat your face with a layer of their saliva. The tongue jabber doesn't kiss. He simply jabs his tongue in and out of your mouth like a woodpecker. It is a complete mystification when you experience any one of these freakish kisses.

I will not tolerate someone who is deceptive or manipulative. Lying is a dealbreaker, no questions asked! If you lie to me, you are out!

Someone who abuses drugs or alcohol will not make it in my world. Having a fun night out with drinks isn't the same as someone who gets blackout drunk on a regular basis or someone that takes prescription drugs to self-medicate every night. If you show up at my house with glassy eyes, are moody, and are slurring at weird hours day or night, you are not my guy.

Hypocrites have no place in my life and will find themselves on the curb at record speed. Taking a holier than now attitude, when you are the biggest violator, will not fly with me. Thinking you are perfect or better than everyone else is the epitome of "not my guy."

A control freak has no place in my life, no questions asked. The worst experiences of my past relationships were due to a controlling partner. I vowed never to allow a controlling person to enter my life again. I swore that brand of crazy off years ago and would never welcome that in again.

If I had to sum it up, my guy must have a job, a car, a house, no young children, a nonsmoker, a good kisser, not a liar, no addictions, not a hypocrite, and not controlling. I will refer to my dates in each chapter as Chad, so the many names don't blur together. Read my stories and use them as a guide when you enter into your own dating adventures and look for the "*red flags.*"

PART 2:

HONORABLE MENTION

CHAPTER 3:

THE LUNCH DATE SCAM

———

It was early in my dating adventures when I noticed a promotion on Groupon from a company called "Dinner Date." The company was a matchmaking service, and the deal offered four separate dates with four compatible matches. The company made all the arrangements surrounding the date, and all I had to do was show up. They were marketing this promotion with a substantial discount, and I couldn't pass it up. *What did I have to lose?*

I hadn't met anyone that rocked my world thus far, so I thought, why not? I signed up for the deal and was enthusiastic about meeting my four dates.

I called the number on the voucher to create my profile and get things started. I spoke to a gentleman named Rick who claimed he was the owner that started the company. We made arrangements to meet in person to fill out the obligatory questionnaire, review my criteria, and ask me a slew of questions to finalize my profile.

Unlike a normal dating site, there are no pictures as a reference in this process. It is truly like going on four blind dates. My fate and success with this particular dating process were going to be determined by this Rick guy collecting all my pertinent information. He told me I could expect my first date arrangement within the next couple of weeks. I smiled, shook his hand, and went on my way with a new confidence and hoped I would find "my guy."

Rick contacted me by email a couple of days later and told me he wanted to review the specifics of my first Dinner Date the following week. I called him and got the low down on Chad, including the time and place to meet.

Dinner Date #1 was with a fifty-year-old widowed man named Chad. Our directions by the Dinner Date personnel were to meet at 6 p.m. at a local restaurant. I was thrilled because the restaurant was a hop, skip, and a jump from my house. I left work a little early to ensure a punctual arrival for my exciting mystery date. I would have arrived on time or even with time to spare but, I hadn't anticipated the severe weather that rolled in, an accident on the highway (not involving me) that caused gridlock, the nonworking traffic light, and a stopped train that blocked the crossing I had to cross to get to my destination. I detoured around the block to avoid the blocked train crossing and called Chad to let him know I would be late. He was very understanding and accommodating about my tardiness.

I arrived at my date thirty minutes later than expected, which really wasn't too bad considering all of the obstacles I encountered. The hostess directed me to the bar, where Chad was seated with a glass of wine. I approached the bar, and the minute he made eye contact, I could tell that Chad wasn't my type. The enthusiasm I felt all day vanished. He wasn't ugly by any means, but he just wasn't my cup of tea, and I didn't find him attractive. I didn't want to be superficial or shallow, so I continued the date with an open mind.

I apologized again for being late. Being late really stressed me out, because in general, I am a very punctual person. It is a big turnoff for me when people are not prompt for a date or engagement.

We ordered drinks and some appetizers and started the normal dating dialogue, which consisted of high-level details about each other. In the first thirty minutes of our "orientation period," I discovered several questionable things about Chad. Chad was a pastor, widowed for three years, had a two-year-old daughter, and wanted to find a woman to settle down with, a woman who would take care of his child. *Red flag*! I didn't have a problem with the widower part, but I wasn't okay with the two-year-old daughter part. Being a baby mama to a man's young child wasn't part of my plan in finding my ideal guy. I had been there, done that with my own children, twenty years prior. This was very important to me, and I was very adamant about this particular topic when completing my initial questionnaire. I didn't understand how Rick missed this very important detail about Chad. This was a deal breaker for me.

Dinner Date #1 was a one and done, and I felt like it was a waste of one of my four dates. Chad being a pastor was a key detail not brought to my attention prior to accepting the date. I wasn't necessarily opposed to this line of work, but he said, "Amen" every time I spoke a word. This was a significant *red flag* for sure. Rick should have asked me if I was open to dating a pastor prior to setting me up on a date with Chad. This could have been a conflict of interest based on my religious beliefs. I would have passed on this date with Chad and could have potentially met someone else.

Needless to say, I didn't go on any more dates with Chad, but I saw him on numerous dates with other women after that. Since my experience with Chad, I made it a rule to confirm a person's occupation, the number of children they have, and the ages of those children prior to going on a date.

Dinner Date #2 was in late October with a gentleman named Chad who managed a famous American rock band that performs across the country during the holidays. The plan was to meet Chad for dinner at a Friday's located close to my work. When I arrived at the table and saw Chad, I was very pleased by his handsomeness. He stood up and said politely, "Hello there, Karen. It's a pleasure to meet you." He gave me a friendly noncommittal hug, smiled, and pulled out my chair for me. This was a rare gesture demonstrated by the men I had been on dates with. We positioned ourselves at the table and started with the normal dating niceties.

Chad had spectacular green eyes, a marvelous head of hair, and stood approximately 5'9." The date appeared promising after the first five minutes until reality hit me. Chad, though very striking, had the temperament of a gnat, the personality of a rock, and no sense of humor whatsoever. I was so disappointed in Chad's inability to hold a normal conversation. The dialogue with him was quite boring, gave me little enjoyment, and was limited to one-to-two-word answers. I think Chad could sense I became disengaged from our date after an hour of tolerating the one-sided banter.

Out of nowhere, he chimed into the discussion, which caught me totally off guard. Chad informed me his American band tour ran from November to February and started the following week. I inquired how he expected us to continue dating if he was traveling for the next four months. *Red flag!*

He responded with one of his short answers, "Not sure!" Clearly, this was the beginning of the end for Dinner Date #2. Once again, I questioned Rick's reasoning behind setting me up on a date with someone who would be gone for four months following our date.

At the end of our date, Chad walked me to my car, like a gentleman, and shook my hand. There was no friendly hug now!

I learned to always inquire about the details of someone's occupation and travel schedule prior to the meeting to ensure I wouldn't be left high and dry after the first date.

Dinner Date #3, they scheduled a lunch date with a guy named Chad. We arranged to meet at a cute little Italian place which was conveniently located five minutes from my work. The Dinner Date team gave me a description of Chad and the specifics of the date. Based on what they told me about Chad, I was anxious to meet him.

It wouldn't be hard to locate Chad at the restaurant since the occupancy was less than twenty people. The moment I walked into the restaurant, I locked eyes with the dark-haired fellow who sat at the back table. I knew it had to be Chad, and he represented his description to a tee. I found him very attractive, and we had an amazing conversation. I was very hopeful with this guy, and I walked out of the restaurant with a smile on my face. He asked to meet up again, and I hoped it would be sooner than later. I thanked him for lunch and an enjoyable time. He told me he would call me later that evening to set up another date, but unfortunately, I never heard from him again. We never exchanged numbers, so I was unable to contact him. I was very disappointed with the outcome of this date. I reached out to the Dinner Date team to get Chad's number, but they explained they weren't allowed to provide a date's phone number without consent, and Chad didn't give consent. I gave consent in the event Chad wanted to contact me, but I wasn't hopeful.

The Final Dinner Date was with a guy named Chad, and the plan was to meet at Carrabba's Restaurant for dinner. I got the typical description of Chad, and I held out hope this last date would prove successful. I got to the restaurant in a timely manner and looked around for a man who fit the description from the Dinner Date team.

I spotted Chad at the bar and made my way over to where he sat. He politely greeted me and introduced himself. He seemed like a pleasant person, but I felt no chemistry with him, not to mention he was shorter than the description they gave me. *Red flag!* I tried to be optimistic, so we sipped wine and munched on some snacks. We exchanged the normal chitchat and attempted to get to know each other.

After our date, Chad was very interested in seeing me again, but unfortunately, I was not. He asked when he could see me again and told him I would circle back with him after checking my schedule. I had no intention of going out with him again but didn't want to hurt his feelings. Chad texted me several times before I told him I met someone and was pursuing that relationship. He understood and told me to contact him should that situation change. I never went out with him again but have seen Chad on several occasions.

At the conclusion of my four dates, Rick emailed me and asked if I wanted to sign up for more dates with a new package? I told him he owed me at least four more comped dates since I felt he misrepresented the experience he described on our initial meeting. He didn't comply with my request, and I was disappointed. I followed up with a nasty gram and told him what I really felt about his scam company. I reviewed each date with him and told him how unhappy I was with the service his said company offered. I told him he didn't set me up with anyone that met the criteria in my profile and had no intention of referring his service to any of my many single friends.

My theory was Rick was a cheat and suckered women into his "Dinner Date" scam and then sets his friends up with the women. It was very clear to me that the essential profile information I provided didn't play a role in matching me with my four dates.

CHAPTER 4:

THE BOOP GUY

——

He introduced himself to me with a firm handshake and situated himself across the table from me. He looked just as dreamy in person as he did in his pictures. He was quite yummy, easy on the eyes, and checked all the boxes for me, which is very uncommon. Was he too good to be true?

We ordered some wine and began to converse. I asked him a couple of questions about himself, and he spent the next twenty minutes responding. He had a very soothing voice, and I enjoyed listening to him speak. When he finished giving me the low down on himself, and gazed into my eyes and said, "So tell me about you, Karen?"

I asked him what he wanted to know?

He fired off ten questions and waited for me to answer. I answered his first question, and he reached over, tapped my nose, and said, "Boop!"

I laughed it off and thought it was cute. I answered the next question, and again I got a "boop" on the tip of my nose. Was he being funny or was this a legit thing? *Red flag!*

It was a legit thing! He tapped my nose and said, "Boop," after everything I said. This wasn't cute at all, and it was annoying as hell. I asked him, "What's with the 'boop' thing?"

He said, "You are so adorable, I can't help myself with a 'boop!'" He was serious. I endured the date to the end but couldn't wait to get the hell out of there. One thousand "boops" in an evening is 999 too many!

I thanked him for a lovely date, and he hugged me. He gave me one final "boop" on the nose for the road. I knew I would never see him again after that and wondered how someone who looked so delicious came with a "boop!"

CHAPTER 5:

THE BLIND GUY

———

I had the strangest date with this guy, and I should have canceled based on the shitty day I had. We met at my favorite little wine bar down the street from me. I had a crazy busy workday, my daughter was sick, and I had tire issues that day! My date was quite the gentleman and stood up to greet me. He gave me a simple hug, and I apologized for being late.

I noticed a vase of flowers on our table, and in hindsight, I never recalled seeing flowers on the tables in my past visits. My date must have noticed the perplexed look on my face and said, "I brought these flowers for you!"

The flowers were a lovely gesture and one that was new to me. I thanked him for the flowers, and he poured me a glass of wine from the bottle he had purchased.

My date blabbed on for the next three hours about the last thirty years of his life, and I couldn't get a word in edgewise. Some of the stories from his "time machine" were interesting, but most were mind-numbing, and I dozed off several times. He shared very little about who he was in his present-day life and kept going back in time. I found this to be very odd.

It caught me off guard when he finally engaged me in the conversation. He asked, "Where do you live?"

I responded, "I live about five minutes from here. I love coming to this place. They have wine tastings on Fridays and Saturdays."

He informed me he only lived ten minutes away and had taken an Uber there.

I made a joke and said, "Did you plan on getting hammered tonight?"

He laughed and said, "Heck no!" He then proceeded to tell me he didn't have a valid driver's license because of revocation. He had a degenerative eye disease and found it difficult to see when he drove. He elaborated on this eye disease and informed me it would eventually lead to blindness. *Red flag!*

I asked, "How long before you go blind?"

He responded, "Ten years or less."

Blindness? I didn't sign up to fall in love with someone who would be blind in the next ten years.

While I processed that piece of information, I wondered how a relationship with him would play out if it were successful, which it wasn't. No license? That meant I would have to drive everywhere, or we have to Uber everywhere for the rest of time? I wasn't down for that game plan.

The bar closed at ten, so I told him to call an Uber for his pickup. He reiterated, "You know, I only live ten minutes away?" He basically hinted for a ride home. I purposedly ignored his "hint" and motioned to his phone for him to call an Uber. No offense, but I don't drive men home after dates, especially a first date!

He waited ten minutes longer before he finally called for his Uber. His estimated pick-up time was twenty minutes. I was so over this date and wanted to go home. The thought of spending another twenty minutes listening to him talk about himself nauseated me.

I said, "Are you okay waiting for your Uber without me? I am super tired and want to get going?"

He looked at me with sad *"puppy dog"* eyes and said, "I will be fine."

I jumped in my car and was out of there in no time flat. He invited me out on another date, but I wasn't interested in the least. I let him down easy and told him I thought he was a great guy, but there was no love connection for me. I wished him well in his search for love.

CHAPTER 6:

MR. JAGGED TEETH

———

Oh my goodness, do I have a story for you. My dating saga continues, and I swear I can't make this shit up. I was so excited to meet this Chad dude. He was a beautiful specimen of a man, and I had chatted with him for several weeks before deciding to meet in person. He was delicious looking, with brilliant blue eyes, athletic build, salt and pepper hair, and was a great dresser. I felt pretty good about this one since we liked many of the same things and had a lot in common. He liked to bike, run, ski, golf, and drink wine! Did I mention he made a great living as a male nurse? So far, he checked all the boxes for me, and it was almost too good to be true.

We met at this little restaurant in Tremont, and I arrived about five minutes early. My date was already sitting at the bar, and I knew who he was because of his distinguished head of hair. He turned around, stood up, and greeted me with a closed-mouth smile. He hugged me and said, "Hello Karen, you look amazing!"

We sat down and ordered some drinks. I started the conversation by telling him how much I loved this quaint restaurant and the happy hour snacks it offered. He turned to me and said, "The brussels sprouts are amazing here."

As he spoke those words, I focused solely on his teeth. They were brown, rotten, jagged, and straight out of a horror movie. I couldn't believe it! Holy crap! It looked like he had lived on a diet of brown rocks and candy his whole life. I thought to myself, how could someone so attractive allow himself to have such horrible mouth hygiene? *Red flag!*

I was awestruck by his deformed teeth and was unable to focus on anything he said from that point forward. I was completely preoccupied and mesmerized by those disgusting teeth. His teeth looked exactly like Christopher Walken's in the Headless Horseman movie. Thank gosh he didn't have the pale face or freaky eyes, or I would have run for the hills. There was no doubt in my mind this is where nightmares come from!

I was oblivious to every single word that came out of his mouth. He could have told me he loved me or asked me to marry him, and I wouldn't have heard him because his gross mouth totally hypnotized me. I could never get past those vile teeth, so there would be no future dates with Chad. The thought of being kissed by that mouth made me gag! The image of his scary brown grin looped over and over in my mind. There is no way I was the first person to react to his teeth like this. He must own a mirror and knows how bad his teeth look.

Chad knew something had changed in my behavior when I cut the date short. He walked me to my car, hugged me, and tried to kiss me. I turned my head, and he kissed me on the cheek. There was no way in hell that rotten mouth was kissing me. He told me he enjoyed meeting me and wanted to know when he could see me again.

I politely said, "I think you are a great guy, but I am not feeling a connection here. I am sorry!"

He looked truly upset and said, "That is disappointing. I thought we really hit it off."

But what I really wanted to say was, "Go see a dentist!"

CHAPTER 7:

THE FISHHOOK KISSER

———

I had been out shopping for the day with my girlfriend, and we decided to stop for dinner on our way back. We ordered a couple of well-deserved glasses of wine while we reviewed the menu. A handsome gentleman was sitting to my right, and he interjected himself into our conversation. He recommended some items on the menu we should consider ordering.

My girlfriend said, "He clearly can afford to patronize this pricy restaurant, so he must do okay for himself. Plus, he's cute, he's not wearing a wedding band, so I think he's single and seems nice!"

He suggested we get a couple of entrées and split them so we could try different things. We had a delicious meal, and our new friend bought us dessert. He asked for my number, so we exchanged information. My friend said she would meet me in the car because I had to visit the restroom.

When I walked out of the restroom, the guy was standing there waiting for me. He wanted to walk me to my car. Halfway to my car, he stopped and said, "I wanted to kiss you from the moment we met!" We kissed for a couple of minutes when suddenly I felt his finger pulling at the corner of my mouth.

Red flag! I thought to myself, "Why is his finger in my mouth?" I had never, in all my experiences, had someone fishhook my mouth while they kissed me! Who does that? I stopped kissing him abruptly and said goodbye.

I truly believe finding a compatible kisser is very important. A person you connect with through a "kiss" can be a wonderful and magical thing. There are many types of kissers out there, and some are not pleasant. A shitty kiss can ruin the moment and wreck the connection, leaving a giant thought bubble above your head with a question mark in it.

I got in the car with my girlfriend and told her about the fishhook kiss.

She laughed and said, "That kind of crazy thing can only happen to you."

We laughed about it the whole way home. He called me several times after that, but I never returned his call.

Was I in the right to be turned off by this horrible gesture during a kiss? Should I have taken his call? Should I be honest with him and tell him how f'd up that finger thing he did was?

CHAPTER 8:

THE GHOST

I was flipping through the many faces on a popular dating app when I came across "The Ghost." I met "The Ghost" for the first time, a year earlier when I was actively dating. Like any Ghost, they had a name, and he was Chad. Chad was my last date that year and also the reason I put dating on hold for the last six months. Let's rewind to my first date with Chad earlier that fall to understand better why I called him "The Ghost."

I was at the end of my "dating" rope last fall when I got a flirt from Chad. A flirt is similar to a "like," swipe right, or a thumbs up! We chatted for a couple of days and scheduled a date for the following week. The next day he texted me to let me know his schedule had changed and suggested we meet up that night. I'm usually open to spontaneity, but I wasn't feeling at the top of my game that particular day. I didn't like what I was wearing or how my hair looked. I felt subpar and was leery about the meeting since first impressions are everything, but I thought, what the hell?

It was evident we both came straight from work as Chad was sporting his work attire. By day he was a plumber and did landscaping as a side hustle.

We both had a couple of drinks and split an appetizer. The conversation was just average, but overall, I was pleasantly surprised by our date. He informed me he was leaving for Florida to visit his brother a couple of days later. I was a little bummed because I hoped we would be able to meet up again soon.

I liked Chad and felt comfortable enough to exchange digits with him, so we could text the week he was gone. I rarely share my cell number this early, as we would typically continue to text on the dating app until things progress in the right direction. I assumed he would reciprocate and send me his number, but he never did. We continued messaging on the dating site for the first half of the week while he was gone.

I wanted to send him a message the next morning, but he was MIA (missing in action)! *Red flag!*

His profile was gone and no longer available for me to view. It ticked me off I couldn't reach out to question his disappearance. It seemed like everything was moving along in the right direction, so I was confused. I figured he met someone in Florida and deleted his profile. A simple message to let me know what happened would have been nice. He totally ghosted me! I think it's rude and inconsiderate when people just disappear without any explanation. That moment, I decided to take a six-month hiatus from dating.

Coincidently, Chad was one of the first people to pop up as a connection and "like" me the first day I got back on dating this time around.

I liked his pictures and was curious if he would respond or simply swipe left and disappear again. I included a quick message that said, "Hi there, I think we went out last fall?"

He responded rather quickly, which surprised me. He also acknowledged the fact we went on a date last fall. We texted back and forth for a bit, and he suggested we meet up for a drink. I accepted his invitation and was curious to learn what his story was last fall.

I felt great, loved how I looked, and was confident in myself for this date. Chad arrived a few minutes before me, and I greeted him at the bar. He eyeballed me from top to bottom, and he wasn't discreet about it. He feasted his eyes on me and seemed very pleased by what he saw. We ordered a couple of drinks and shared some appetizers. I enjoyed our time and decided to postpone my inquiry about his disappearing act from last fall. I would broach that topic another time.

The bar was closing earlier than normal due to COVID-19, so we tried to come up with a plan B so the evening didn't have to end.

I rarely invited a guy to my house or let him know where I lived this early in courting, but I offered going to my place for a nightcap. I broke my rule for some odd reason that night but was fairly confident he wasn't a serial killer.

It was a beautiful evening, and we sat by the firepit with a glass of wine. We picked up the conversation where we left off. Chad leaned in and gave me a kiss! The kiss was a little disappointing. We never kissed last fall, but I had bigger *"kiss expectations"* from a good-looking guy like him. His lips resembled a stiff fish mouth. It wasn't the worst kiss I had ever experienced, but it wasn't anywhere close to the best.

He got up after five minutes and said, "I have an early day tomorrow and need to get going." His abrupt exit was strange. I showed him to the door, gave him a small peck kiss, and said good night.

I left him a message thanking him for an enjoyable evening and gave him my number to set up our next date. He never responded to my message that evening, and I figured he went straight to bed. The next day came, and a reply never came because he had ghosted me again. *Red flag!*

CHAPTER 9:

ANOTHER PLAN MAN

———

My date looked like a college history professor because he was wearing man jeans, a light brown dress shirt, a sport jacket with leather patches on the elbows, and brown "dad-like" loafers. He was 6' tall, attractive, with warm brown eyes, and a thick head of brownish-gray hair.

The third time the bartender asked if we wanted to order any food, Chad looked at me and said, "Nothing for me. I'm doing an intermittent fasting diet."

I asked, "What does that mean?"

He explained he was only allowed to eat during certain hours of the day, and the rest of the time, he fasted. It's always awkward when my date doesn't eat when I am starving. He looked at me and said, "If you are hungry, get something."

I ordered the crispy brussels sprouts, which consisted of four in the bowl when they arrived. I offered Chad one of my brussels sprouts, and he said, "I hate brussels sprouts!" I ate my four small brussels sprouts in less than ten minutes and was still hungry.

I couldn't help but notice that Chad kept looking at his watch the entire forty-five minutes we were there. I asked him in a joking way, "Is there somewhere you have to be? You keep looking at your watch?" *Red flag!*

Chad disclosed he had tickets for a concert that evening.

I said, "You have tickets for a concert tonight? Don't most concerts start at 7 p.m.? ˊ What time were you planning to leave?"

He replied, "Do you want to join me?"

"Umm, NO!" I wasn't getting into a car with someone I just met, much less going to a concert. I politely said, "I appreciate the offer, but we only met you forty-five minutes ago and don't feel comfortable going to a concert with you." I've seen too many Lifetime movies and didn't want to end up kidnapped or chopped up in little pieces scattered from there to the concert venue. I told him we would touch base in a couple of days and enjoy the concert. I hardly got the sentence out, and he was gone.

I shook my head and thought, *what the hell?*

Little did I know my evening would go "from suck to blow" after that and provide content for another chapter in my book! My night began with a "fasting guy" who had another plan, to being subjected to an overbearing, smitten, narcissist, who referred to me as his next "ex-wife," who sent me home with enough food for three days. I seriously couldn't make this shit up if I tried.

CHAPTER 10:

FROM SUCK TO BLOW

———

I was still hungry after eating four brussels sprouts on my earlier date and headed to a restaurant close by to get a real meal. I contorted my body to get into the one remaining spot at the bar. I got settled in my seat and felt someone's hand on my shoulder. A deep voice said, "A beautiful woman like you shouldn't eat dinner in this cramped space. Come with me, and I will get you a proper table." I turned and saw a bald man, who I presumed to be the manager.

I manipulated my way out of that shitty seat and followed the bald man to the hostess stand. The kind man said, "Wait here, while I find you a spot." A couple of minutes later, he returned and said, "Follow me." He directed me back to the same spot I had just come from. The couple sitting next to me left, so their seats opened up.

I questioned why the bartender set a place for two people, and before I could comprehend the situation, the bald guy plopped himself down next to me. He introduced himself as Chad and handed me his business card. I reciprocated the gesture and gave him my business card. I realized he was not the manager, just a guy at the bar.

Chad was probably ten years older, stood 5'9," and was well dressed. He wasn't unattractive, but I wasn't drawn to him in the least. He was very overconfident, and it was clear he thought he was God's gift to women. He was a very successful realtor in the area, and he was very conceited, arrogant, and pompous. I personally found his demeanor to be a huge turnoff! The way he talked, and carried himself, was annoying. *Red flag!*

He was a legacy in his own mind!

I just wanted to get something to eat and go home, but now I found myself detained by this stranger. The evening seemed like it was never going to end.

This is where the night got weird. He ordered a bottle of the "Purple Cowboy" cabernet, which happened to be his second of the evening. He yammered on and on about everyone and everything he knew. Two glasses of wine are my limit, so I knew I'd only have one glass. He guzzled down three-quarters of that bottle of wine in the blink of an eye. The only words he spoke that stuck in my mind from that night were, *"You are going to be my next ex-wife."*

Who says that? He was very smitten by me and felt the need to impress.

He asked me what I wanted for dinner.

I said, "I just came here to get a steak and go home."

He said, "Do you like lobster bisque?"

I said, "Yes, I do!"

He ordered me a cup of lobster bisque, a filet, and something for himself. He directed the servers around like he owned them. I am sure the servers hate when people talked to them in this manner, but I am certain his gratuity was well worth any aggravation he caused. I just wanted to get the fuck out of there and go home. I was stuck in my own hell.

My dinner came, and I ate a couple of bites of my steak and ended up taking the rest of it home. He never touched his meal and told the server to wrap it with my stuff. He made sure they threw in a couple of extra cups of lobster bisque and a dessert. I went from hardly getting fed on my previous date to bringing home enough food for the next couple of nights.

I made my exit strategy and started to head out. I parked my car about four spots down from the restaurant's exit. I tried to make my way to the door quickly, and Chad was unexpectedly right behind me. He insisted on driving me to my car. I pointed to my car, which was fifteen feet from where I stood. I said, "You already walked me to my car." The bottom line was he wanted to show me he drove a fancy car to try to impress me further. I wasn't impressed, just annoyed because I wanted to leave, and this guy had turned into a stage five clinger. *Red flag!* I pretended to be awestruck by his vehicle, but I couldn't care less by his outdated Benz. Little did he know, I grew up in a yuppie town, where prestigious cars were run of the mill, and his car would be considered passé.

I turned to leave for the third time, and he stopped me once again and asked me if I was okay to drive, which I was. I wanted to reverse the question on him but knew it would just delay my departure even further. He pulled out this little bottle and squirted some liquid in his mouth. He told me it was mint and offered me some, which I declined. Chad loved affirmation for his generous gestures because they made him feel illustrious. He said goodbye and said, "I will call you tomorrow, but know I never call a woman twice."

I am not really sure what that meant, but I didn't care. What a cluster this evening had been.

"*This could only happen to you, Karen,*" I muttered to myself as I started my car and made my way home.

When I got home, my daughter was sitting at the kitchen table doing homework and asked, "How did your date go? Did you get fed?"

I laughed out loud, lifted up the bags of food I was holding, and said, "Fasten your seatbelt, girl! Man, do I have a crazy ass story for you." I revisited the events of the evening with her, and before long, we were both laughing hysterically.

After that date, I promised myself I would always order food on a date if I was hungry. If I ever found myself in a similar situation with a guy like Chad, I would remove myself immediately from that situation instead of being polite and tolerating it until the end.

PART 3:

ONE AND DONE, OR TWO

CHAPTER 11:

A LEGACY IN MY OWN MIND

———

I was wearing heels and a cute little skirt, not my running shoes and shorts. I quickly exited the restaurant and beelined for my car. In my mind, I was escaping a serial killer, so my adrenaline was at an all-time high. I got to the parking garage and ran up the stairs in my heels. When I got to the top floor, I was anxious to see my car, but my car wasn't there! *What? Where is my car?*

I looked around and saw that my car was on the rooftop of the parking garage adjacent to where I was standing. I thought about taking the elevator but hesitated to push the button. *What if Chad already paid and left the restaurant? What if the elevator doors opened and he is standing there?* With a flurry of crazy thoughts running through my mind, I opted to take the stairs. Down I went, trying not to fall. I hurried to the other garage and scurried up the stairs to the rooftop. I opened the door to feast my eyes on my beautiful black Honda CRV. I got in, locked the doors, and yelled Hallelujah!

I called my friend Becky on my way home and asked her about Chad. She informed me she used to babysit for Chad's family, and he used to physically abuse his wife. *Red flag!* Needless to say, I understood why he didn't want me talking to Becky about him. Becky called it a blessing in disguise.

Let's backtrack to where this bizarre and preposterous date with Chad began.

It was midsummer, and I had been chatting with this guy named Chad for a week before deciding it was time to meet. He seemed relatively normal, from what I could tell from our texts and the quick five-minute conversation we had. He was a handsome man with a big head of dark hair, a nice smile, and beautiful blue eyes. From the pictures posted on his profile, he appeared to be a nice dresser and lived in a quaint home. We met at a new Italian place I wanted to try at 5:30 p.m. The plan was to have dinner, walk around Crocker Park, and then go to a movie.

It was a beautiful evening, and the temperature was perfect. I was wearing a sleeveless linen shirt with a navy sweater, a short cotton plaid skirt, and cute white heels. I got to the restaurant about ten minutes early and was seated at a table with an umbrella outside on the patio.

I sat there anticipating Chad's arrival when an obnoxious noise sidetracked me. I looked to my left and noticed a rusty red pickup truck with an extremely loud muffler pulling into the parking lot. I somehow knew my date had arrived. A nice-looking man, wearing a trendy shirt, and nice dress shorts, got out of the vehicle. This man resembling Chad was walking toward the entrance of the restaurant. I braced myself for impact.

The hostess brought Chad out to the patio, where I was waiting. I stood up to introduce myself, and he reached out his hand to shake mine. I put my hand out, and in one fell swoop, he grabbed me, twirled me in, and gave me a giant bear hug. This gesture totally caught me off guard, as it did the hostess based on the wide-eyed, mortified look on her face. He sat down at the end of the table, and I positioned myself at a comfortable distance to his right.

I carried the majority of the conversation with little or no input from my date. When I attempted to solicit an answer from him, all he would say was, "I like you, seriously, I like you!" This response occurred over and over again for the next hour. At one point, while I was in the middle of talking, he barked out two new words, "Move closer!"

Before I knew what happened, he said, "Move closer" once again, reached over, grabbed the leg of my chair, and moved me within four inches of his chair. I found this abrupt gesture to be very odd and unexpected. *Red flag!*

When he pulled this stunt for a second time, I quickly warned him to stop or I would leave. I repositioned my chair and patiently waited for my dinner to arrive.

Our dinners arrived, and we began to eat. I welcomed the break from the awkward conversation. I had just taken my second bite when Chad lunged over, grabbed my face, and tried to make out with me. My mouth was full of seafood pasta when he attempted to shove his tongue down my throat. I pulled back in horror and said, "What the hell are you doing? You are being very aggressive for a first date, and I don't like it." *Red flag!*

He replied, "I like you!"

I knew there would be no second date for Chad and wanted to get through this one and done date!

The only time Chad contributed to our conversation was when we discovered he knew my friend Becky. Becky was a good friend and a work colleague of mine. He quickly diverted the conversation to the server and asked for the check. He then looked me straight in the eyes and said in a very stern tone, "If you mention anything about me or this date to Becky, I will hunt you down and hit you in the head with a two-by-four!" *Red flag!* There was a long awkward pause, and then he started laughing hysterically!

"What the hell? Did he really just say that? Who the hell says this to someone on a date?"

I didn't know what to think about his strange comment about Becky but knew I would be calling her after this date. I didn't react because I was still in shock from the words that came out of his mouth. I simply chuckled, like it was a joke, but this was no joke! This guy was a freak!

When I tell people this story, they ask, "Why didn't you just leave and walk out of the restaurant?" I don't know why I didn't do that. In hindsight, I wish I had left immediately. That was the logical thing to do, but I didn't. I was afraid of Chad and what his reaction would be if I just walked out. *Would he follow me home and stalk me? Did he really have a two-by-four in that rusty red truck? Would he fly off the handle and go crazy?* My mind flooded with a litany of scenarios of how this this date could end. I was suddenly living my own Lifetime TV movie.

I mentally created a strategy to escape this shitty date. Chad told me to follow him to Crocker Park, and we would go from there. I pretended to be on board with the plan, but I had a different game plan in my mind. When he turned right to Crocker Park, I would pause, turn left, and speed away to safety. This part didn't play out the way I had hoped. He drove so slowly I was practically attached to his bumper. This was his way to ensure he didn't lose me on the three-minute drive to Crocker Park. My escape plan didn't go as I had hoped, so I had to rethink my strategy.

Plan B involved the timing of stoplights. I would put some space between our cars and hoped one of the two stoplights would allow Chad to make it through and turn red for me. I would make a U-turn and speed away safely. This scenario didn't happen the way I envisioned either, as neither of the lights changed in my favor, and I was still following this clown to Crocker.

Plan C had to be put in motion. If this one didn't work, I was shit out of luck. The date was to include dinner, walking around Crocker, and a movie. Clearly, there was no movie in my future with Chad. I would suggest stopping for a glass of wine at Brio, which was an amazing Italian bistro with a charming outdoor patio. The plan was to position myself at Brio with a glass of wine and then sneak out gracefully, unbeknownst to my date. This whole fucked up date was playing out like a scary movie in my mind, and I was the girl trying to escape my own scene.

We parked on the top level of the parking garage and headed to Brio for a glass of wine. During our walk to Brio, Chad attempted several times to plant one of those disgusting kisses on me. The thought of another toilet bowl kiss grossed me out! I pushed him away and reminded him I didn't appreciate his aggressiveness. We finally arrived at Brio, where we were seated at a high-top table outside, and ordered a couple of glasses of wine. I felt like I was worthy of a shot or seven of tequila.

We waited for our drinks to arrive when out of nowhere, Chad began to sneeze incessantly. It wasn't bad enough that he sneezed no less than twenty times, but he never covered his mouth. I was so embarrassed at the slop that flew out of his mouth during his sneezing episode. He looked like a St. Bernard shaking off after a bath in slow motion. A woman at an adjacent table shot me a death stare because she was so appalled by Chad's repulsive saliva spectacle. I looked at her and motioned with an innocent look that screamed *I am on a bad date!*

The server brought our wine, and I finally saw the light at the end of the nightmare date tunnel. I enjoyed half of my wine before I excused myself to the restroom. I went into the restaurant and immediately found our server Mike. I asked him if I could sneak out the back door, through the kitchen, like you see in movies. He questioned my motivation to sneak out the back door. I enlightened him on the craziness of the bad date I was on, and I needed to leave. He gave me a per-plexed look because he thought we were newlyweds, based on how my date kept trying to hold my hand. He informed me there was no door in the kitchen for me to escape but offered up the front door as a means for me to flee. I begged Mike, the server, not to bring the check to my date for at least ten to fifteen minutes, even if my date asked for it. I needed time to get to my car and leave before he realized I was not coming back. That is when I escaped out the front door of the establishment and fled to my car.

I got a message from Chad the next day as expected. He questioned the reasoning for my departure. He asked me why I left him at the restaurant without notice. I quickly revisited the evening and explained point by point all the things he did wrong from the minute he sat down at the restaurant.

I wished him well in his search to find a partner and hung up. I immediately blocked him on the dating site and my cell phone.

The next time I returned to that restaurant, I sought out Mike to thank him for saving the day. I shared the high-level details of my date, and he totally understood why I left him there. I asked Mike how long it took for "the dude" to realize I wasn't coming back from the restroom. Mike said the guy got up and went by the restrooms after about fifteen minutes. He saw Mike and asked if he had seen me. Mike informed him he saw me leave a while ago. Mike divulged he regularly shared my story with patrons, and I was a Brio Legend. Mike and I still chuckle about this story to this day.

I promised myself if I were ever in a similar situation, I would stand up and remove myself from the date immediately.

CHAPTER 12:

THE SORE LOSER

He was a sore fucking loser! Chad couldn't stand the fact a woman beat him at a silly game of pool. I regularly listen to my friend's crazy dating experiences and feel quite fortunate there was only one time in ten years my date left me high and dry mid-date.

My dating adventure with Chad started in a normal manner. It began with lots of messaging the first week and progressed to talking on the phone the following. Chad had a sexy phone voice, and I loved hearing him talk. I make it clear to guys I start conversing with I am not a phone talker. I am good for fifteen minutes maximum, and that's it. Chad's voice was very soothing, and I could actually listen to him for hours but didn't.

Chad was very cute and was my type. He was on the taller side, had a great body, was in amazing shape, had lots of thick dark hair, and yummy brown eyes. He was well-groomed and nicely dressed in all of his profile pictures. I looked for attributes like this in a potential partner. Chad made a lucrative living as an electrician, had no kids, and was married once before, for a short time. There weren't any *red flags* that would derail me from meeting him in person at this point. We decided to meet and set the plan in motion.

We talked about different options and couldn't decide, so I said, "I am going to let you pick the place. Just let me know where and when." I like to let my date pick the place to meet on a first date because it gives me a good read on what kind of foodie they are and how deep their wallet is.

First impressions are everything, and their choice of restaurant tells me a lot about a guy!

Chad pondered for days on the location for us to meet. He raved about a fancy new pizza place in North Olmsted he wanted to try. He explained how they recently restored it after a grease fire, so it wasn't really "new." Chad was adamant the pizza place would be the location of our first date.

I was an avid foodie, and loved to try different restaurants, so how had I not heard of this so-called *infamous* restaurant? I racked my brain trying to figure out how such a renowned restaurant had eluded me? I felt like I had tried every pizza place in Ohio since moving here from Chicago. Not dissimilar to my dating adventures in search of a decent man. I was excited to discover this new *covert* pizza place.

I was punctual to our date and arrived about five minutes early. When I pulled up to this storefront location, I realized I had heard of this place but had never eaten there before. This place was not my typical date locale. It didn't look fancy at all from the outside.

Chad arrived five minutes after me while I was still sitting in my car. Chad waved and got out of his car. He greeted me and we went into the pizza joint together. I wasn't sure why Chad considered this restaurant fancy or upscale, but it couldn't be further from the truth.

Being the marketing professional I was, I struggled to understand the owner's strategy behind promoting this venue Chad referred to as upscale and classy. Unless you were familiar with this restaurant and its location, you wouldn't know it existed. I hadn't seen the inside yet but hoped the outside wasn't representative of what I would find. Maybe this was truly a hidden gem!

The inside left something to be desired and wasn't anything to write home about. It reminded me of an old, outdated Italian restaurant my family frequented when I was a kid. The dark wood booths ran along the sidewalls and screamed 1960s decor. A maroon-colored vinyl material covered the booth seats, which stuck to any exposed skin. Five dark wood, four-top tables filled the center space between the booth-lined walls. The chairs had a dark patterned upholstery with a thick, gaudy, curtain-like material. A metal caddie with parmesan cheese and a set of salt and pepper shakers sat in the middle of each table. It was a dark, uninviting atmosphere, and from the lighting to the decor, it reminded me of something out of a Mafia movie.

The hostess sat us at a booth, and we proceeded with some small talk. We enjoyed a drink and perused the menu to determine what we wanted to order for dinner. Chad decided we were getting pizza, and ordering a separate entrée was *not* an option. I wasn't opposed to pizza, but I thought it was odd how he just made that decision on his own. I had never been on a dinner date before where my date controlled what we were having without question. *Red flag!*

While we ate our pizza, Chad inquired about our plans after dinner. He suggested karaoke or playing pool as the two possibilities to consider.

I chuckled and said, "I am not interested in karaoke, but I am game if that is what you want to do, but you will be singing alone!" I told him I preferred to play pool.

He was cool with my choice to play pool but informed me the venue was in a sketchy area. He gave me the details of the location, and it was not rough in the least. Maybe that was his way to deter me from playing pool because deep down inside he wanted to do karaoke.

He then questioned, "Are you any good at pool?"

I let him know I used to play quite a bit back in college, but clearly, it had been a long time since I played. He seemed relieved to learn I hadn't played in a long time. I asked him if he was a pool shark, and he told me he was decent.

This *sketchy* pool hall was only a couple of blocks from the *upscale, classy restaurant* where we had dinner. We arrived at the bar, and it was a bit of a dive bar, but it wasn't in a questionable part of town. I felt completely safe and didn't feel in danger. We entered the darkish venue and realized all the pool tables were in use. Chad put quarters on the pool table to hold our spot in line to play. We took a seat at the bar, ordered drinks, and waited for one of the two tables to open up.

Chad bragged about what a great pool player he was while we waited our turn. There were two biker-looking dudes at the one table and two burnout-looking fellas at the other. He kept looking at the pool tables and saying, "I can't wait to play. I know I can beat either of those mopes!"

Wow, he certainly had a cocky attitude. *Red flag!* I reiterated I hadn't played in many years, so I wouldn't be the secret weapon to being victorious.

It was finally our turn to play, and we made our way over to the table where the two biker dudes were playing. The names of our opponents were Ralph and Jim. They weren't intimidating at all and were very friendly. I was nervous yet anxious to bring my out-of-date pool playing skills to the game. It was finally our turn, and I let Chad go first. He took his turn and managed to get only one ball in the pocket before his turn was over. I was up next after Ralph's turn. I picked up my pool cue and gave it a good rub with the blue chalk. I took a deep breath and smack went the balls. Surprisingly, I did well on my first turn and got four solid balls into the side pockets.

Chad's second turn proved to be unsuccessful and quite awkward. He wasn't able to get a single ball in a pocket. He had this strange scowl on his face and huffed back to his chair.

I looked at him and said, "Don't worry about it. We are just here to have fun."

He looked at me with daggers in his eyes and said, "Whatever, bitch!"

I couldn't identify what he mumbled, but I swear he called me a *bitch*. *Red flag!*

He was clearly impacted by his inability to play pool like the rock star he portrayed himself to be. He wasn't tooting his own horn now!

My game was on fire, and I was impressed with how well I played. During my next turn, I managed to clear the table and win the game for Chad and me. I looked up to give Chad a high five, but he was nowhere around. I scanned the bar with my eyes, and still no Chad. *He was missing in action!* The biker dudes saw Chad go to the bathroom during my turn, and he hadn't returned. I glanced toward the bathroom and waited for Chad to come out, but he didn't.

I glanced out the front window because I thought maybe he went outside to blow off some steam. At that moment, I saw Chad's car screeching out of the parking lot like he had just robbed a bank. I checked with the bartender to ensure he didn't stick me with the bar tab. He did not!

She told me he said, "That bitch embarrassed the shit out of me by beating me at pool! Fuck her!"

I told her I was on a first date with him, and he just left without saying a word. I couldn't believe Chad left the way he did. I had never experienced such nonsense before. What just happened here? Thank goodness I drove myself to this date, or I would have had to Uber home.

The biker dudes were taken aback by the events that just happened before their eyes. I wasn't going to let that freak ruin my evening. I was having a nice time, despite Chad's childish behavior, and I ended up playing several more rounds of pool with the biker dudes.

When I woke up the next morning, I was still in disbelief about the *"Chad vanishing."* I reviewed the events of the evening over and over again in my mind and couldn't figure out where it went awry. I never reached out to Chad to determine the rationale behind his attitude and disappearance. I never heard another word from Chad and have never seen him out and about since.

I concluded that overly competitive men have no place in my life. Good riddance, Chad! May men like you be *missing in action* from my life forever.

CHAPTER 13:

BAIT AND SWITCH

———

I am a firm believer that age is just a number, but in the case of Chad, I can tell you that's a lie. My story represents a perfect example of bait and switch in the dating world.

I walked into the hotel lobby and looked around for a person who looked like the man in Chad's profile pictures. I heard someone say my name and turned to find a small, older man I didn't recognize. He was a smaller version of the Chad I saw online and was at least fifteen years older. He didn't look like the person I thought I was meeting.

He introduced himself and gave me a loose hug.

I said, "I walked right by you because I didn't recognize you from your pictures. How old are you, really?"

He brushed it off by saying, "I always say I'm fifteen years younger, or I wouldn't attract beautiful women like you."

I questioned, "Don't you think that is deceptive?"

He just shrugged his shoulders and didn't care. He clearly misrepresented himself, and I didn't like that at all. *Red flag!*

I was ready to pull the plug on something that never started, but for some crazy reason, I decided to go to dinner with him anyway. I could certainly be amicable for a couple of hours in exchange for a delicious Blue Point dinner. I enjoyed our conversations prior to being misled, so I figured what the hell, how hard could it be to converse with him at dinner while overlooking his age?

Chad kept engaging random people while we waited for our table. He would say, "This is our first date, and hopefully her last with anyone other than me! I drove here all the way from Michigan to meet this beautiful lady, and she's the one!" We ended up having a relatively nice evening, all things considered, and at the end of the evening, he kept telling me how much he liked me. I had no intention of seeing Chad again after that night. He was a one and done!

The next morning Chad called me from his hotel and asked me if I wanted to join him for breakfast. I declined his offer and told him I had a migraine. I didn't have a migraine but had no desire to meet up with him again. He was deceptive about his age, and that is a deal breaker for me. I let him know I wasn't attracted to him and felt he was dishonest by misrepresenting himself. I thanked him for a lovely evening and wished him well.

Let's backtrack to where this all started.

Chad's pictures on his profile represented a man who was five years older than me, average height, balding on top with graying hair, well-groomed graying beard, laugh lines around his eyes, and normal weight. I communicated with Chad for a couple of weeks before I learned he lived in Michigan.

He gave the impression he lived in Ohio, but in reality, he lived in Michigan and regularly worked in Ohio. *He was geographically undesirable!* I was not open to dating someone from Michigan and wasn't looking for long-distance love. *Red flag!*

Chad assured me he would move heaven and earth to spend time with me if we hit it off. I was anxious to meet this man who was willing to drive all the way from Michigan just to meet me. I made dinner reservations at a nice upscale restaurant of my choice, and we agreed to meet at his hotel and go to dinner from there.

I always confirm a man's age prior to going on a date and use my experience with Chad to justify my inquiry. I also make it a point to verify a man's place of residence, so I don't exceed my thirty-mile max distance rule!

CHAPTER 14:

TWO BOTTLE GUY

———

I wasted six weeks of my life dating a crazy narcissist and needed to get back in the saddle to redeem my faith in men. I made an agreement with myself to jump back into dating for one month, and not a day longer! I figured what happens, happens! There are times when my heart needs to heal after a breakup and times when healing isn't necessary at all. Sometimes, I just need to start dating immediately to regain my self-confidence and make up for wasted time with an asshole. I hit it off with five guys right off the bat, so I was very optimistic, and it was exactly what the doctor ordered.

I lined up dates with each of these gentlemen to see if there was any connection. Let the serial dating begin!

Chad was tall and relatively handsome based on his profile pictures. From what I could tell, he seemed nice and was quite the wine connoisseur. I considered myself a wine snob, but Chad knew his shit about wine, so right out of the gate, we had a connection. We had several common interests like golf, biking, and travel, so we decided to meet.

I like to let my date pick the location of a first date because it helps level-set the degree of cheapness to expect. I mentioned this tactic in a previous chapter.

Chad picked a cute, little Italian restaurant that was the midpoint for both of us. I arrived a little early and made my way into the bar area, where I found Chad. This appeared to be a regular watering hole for Chad, based on all the greetings he got from the staff. He represented his pictures to a tee and was even cuter in person. Chad crossed his legs femininely and was very animated with his hands when he told stories. His soft masculine voice and flamboyant mannerisms were a bit strange to me. *Red flag!*

He ordered up a bottle of white wine before I could utter a word and then said, "Is that okay with you?"

I replied, "I'm more of a red wine girl, but I'm flexible."

Chad quickly countered, "I will order a bottle of red as well."

Two bottles of wine? The bartender poured us each a glass of the white wine, and we toasted our introduction.

My limit when I am driving is two drinks, so I nursed my first glass of wine for an hour and was ready for the red option. Chad said, "Would you like to try the red one?"

I said, "Yes, I would, but that will be my last one tonight!" I explained my two-glass limit, and he just rolled his eyes.

He ordered a bottle of red wine and said, "You can take home what we don't finish."

I liked the sound of that!

Chad finished the remaining bottle of white wine and moved on to the red one. I hoped I would get to take some of the red bottle home, but he gulped it down like it was water. I was perplexed by the way he guzzled wine down. I was at my limit and knew when I finished my red wine I would move on to water.

Chad motioned to the bartender and ordered up two chocolate martinis.

I looked at him and said, "Don't order one for me. I am done after this glass of wine." Once again, he looked at me, smiled, and rolled his eyes.

An older man walked into the bar area and struck up a conversation with Chad. When the man walked away, Chad informed me it was the owner of the restaurant. It was obvious he was a regular here if he was on a friendly basis with the owner. The owner signaled to the server and said, "Get them a martini on me!" When the martinis came, I took a very little sip just to taste it. Chad finished both martinis in record time, and the bartender brought over the two martinis the owner bought!

Chad managed to drink those martinis too! I asked him, "Are you driving home from here?"

He said he was fine to drive home and rationalized it by saying he put ice cubes in his white wine to stay hydrated. How crazy was his thinking? He was an adult, so I couldn't tell him what to do.

We talked about the different golf courses we had played in the area and also about the kinds of wines we liked. He was more relaxed after a couple of glasses of wine and revealed some personal details about himself, which triggered some *red flags*. Thus far was his excessive consumption of alcohol and his odd feminine mannerisms were *red flags*.

We chatted and texted a lot over the next week. The dialogue seemed normal and was comfortable. I decided to give him another chance to prove if he was worthy of dating me. I wanted to set our next date sooner than later to see if this guy had potential. I didn't want to waste time pursuing him if I didn't see a future.

We planned another date, and he picked the place right away. Chad picked a location that was more convenient for him than me, and this was very telling. A good guy picks a place somewhere in the middle or more convenient for the woman versus himself. The fact he picked a place ten minutes from his house and fifty minutes from mine was inconsiderate. *Red flag!*

There was a horrible thunderstorm the day of our second date, and I debated about going. I am terrified of thunder and lightning and hate to drive in a storm! If I canceled the date, I wouldn't be able to meet up with Chad for several weeks because my serial dating schedule was pretty full at the moment. I decided to meet Chad and drive fifty minutes in a thunderstorm.

I set off on my voyage to Solon and braced myself for a white-knuckle drive. The drive was worse than I had envisioned, and cars spun out all around me. I questioned my judgment to go on this date. I considered turning around at least seven times during my drive. The drive took ninety minutes when it normally would take fifty. I arrived at the restaurant and went in to meet Chad.

I walked in, shook off the rain, and saw Chad sitting there with a half-empty bottle of white wine. I sat down and told him how crazy my drive was. I said, "I saw five cars hydroplane and spin off the road right in front of me." I told him I contemplated turning around numerous times during my drive to meet him. I hoped he appreciated my effort to make this date. He didn't give a crap about my scary journey and jumped into a conversation about himself. *Red flag!*

The bartender asked me what I wanted to drink, and I asked, "What kind of cabernet do you have?"

Chad piped up and said, "You can have a glass of mine if you want." I wasn't feeling it for white wine and passed on his offer. Chad suggested I get a bottle of Quilt since bottles were 25 percent off that night. Quilt happened to be one of my favorites, but I didn't want to indulge on a sixty-dollar bottle of wine. Chad directed the bartender to put the bottle of Quilt on his tab and said, "Take home what you don't finish." I was relieved when I heard that! Chad finished his bottle of white wine and ordered another one. He told me he came to this particular bar every Monday and always drank two bottles of this white wine.

Chad suggested going on a weekend getaway to celebrate our birthdays, which happened to be in the same month. *"A weekend getaway together? Was he kidding?"* We had only been on two dates, and we were ready to spend a weekend together? That was too soon for me! I dismissed him by saying, "Unfortunately, I am booked solid for the next month."

Chad asked if I had any pets, and I told him I had a ten-pound dog. He didn't have a dog but said he would love to get one. He poked fun at people who let their dogs sleep in their beds and was adamant he would not tolerate that. I responded by saying, "My little ten-pound dog has slept in my bed almost her whole life."

He grimaced and said, "Hell no!" This was a deal breaker, and it solidified my decision about no third date with Chad. *Red flag!*

I finished my second glass of wine and wanted to leave. The server bagged up my remaining bottle of wine, which I was excited to finish at home. We said our goodbyes, and I left.

I was distant and evasive with Chad for the next several days, which made him wonder what was going on. He left me a nasty voicemail the following week, in which he rambled on about the amazing connection we had but thought it was disgusting my dog slept in my bed. He said, "What is wrong with women in their 50s who let their dogs sleep with them? It's unacceptable!"

Needless to say, I became very aware of how much alcohol a guy consumes on a date after that night. Two bottles and four martinis are too many without question. A guy who can't accept my dog will never last in my life and will be kicked to the curb.

CHAPTER 15:

THE SOFT TALKER

———

I recently met a guy named Chad, and I thought he was pretty nice. He was a couple of years older, had an attractive face, deep dimples, green eyes, and a big head of salt and peppered hair. We messaged for about a week before I felt comfortable enough to meet him. Chad had never been married or had children and those were the only immediate *red flags*. I kept an open mind and stayed the course.

He lived an hour away but agreed to drive the further distance to meet me, which I thought was nice. Chad arrived early because he wanted to ensure he was punctual, and I reminded him I worked until five.

Chad was very polite and greeted me with a complimentary hug. He reeked of bourbon and seemed a little buzzed. He said, "You look incredibly beautiful, and I am so happy to make your acquaintance." I never expected the voice that came out of this burly, broad-shouldered man. He had the deepest, yet softest, yet quietest, womanly voice I had ever heard, and it didn't match up with his masculine physique.

I ordered a glass of cabernet and started the normal dating banter. Chad's voice was very sweet, in a calming way, and listening to his monotone chatter made me want to curl up with a blanket and go to sleep. Regardless of how soothing his voice was, I don't know if I could listen to that voice for the rest of my life and couldn't imagine what he would sound like during a passionate moment.

Chad ordered a couple of appetizers and had a couple of more bourbons. He was soused and was slurring his words, so I was glad he ate some food. I was concerned he had to drive an hour back home and hoped he would sober up.

Was he just nervous or what? He scarfed down the appetizers like he hadn't eaten in a week. He spent the next thirty minutes talking about all of the places he wanted to take me on special getaways. He said, "I can see us making love at sunrise while listening to the waves crash on the beach outside the window." He had us walking hand in hand on the beach at sunset and fantasized about these trips in such great detail, and it creeped me out. *Red flag!*

"Hello, this is our first date!"

I would love all the things he offered, but this was way too much to grasp on a first date. He's the guy that expected to move in together after four months or the guy who thought you were exclusive after the second date. This fast-moving pace sent me running to the hills!

Chad had a sparkle in his eye and was very enamored with me by the end of the night. How could he help himself, right? Unfortunately, the feelings weren't mutual, and there would not be another date or fantasy trips. He wanted to set up our next date, and I gave my canned answer, "I will have to check my schedule and get back to you."

I hated confrontation and avoided it at all costs, especially when it came to dead-end dates. I established this exit strategy early on in dating because of disgruntled dates with men who didn't take rejection well. This allowed me to safely escape a date and drop the bad news on them later.

Chad texted me nonstop over the next couple of days until I couldn't take it any longer. I was forthcoming with the dreaded news and let him know I wasn't feeling a connection with him. He sent me pictures from his vacation and urged me to reconsider my position about us. When I am done, I am done.

I will run for the hills every single time a guy comes on too strong and gets serious too quickly. I liked he was punctual but struggled with him being hammered when I arrived. There was no discipline to drink responsibly. A guy that messages me incessantly gets blocked immediately because that is a sign of cray-cray!

PART 4:

THREE STRIKES YOU'RE OUT

CHAPTER 16:

ISN'T HE PRETTY?

Chad and I met at a restaurant close to the fundraiser location. We had a very enjoyable meal and conversation. Once we finished dinner, we made our way to the event. The fundraiser was for a good friend's four-year-old granddaughter fighting cancer. I contributed several gift baskets containing miscellaneous gift packaging, party goods, stickers, and stationery for auction items at the event.

I historically don't make a practice of bringing a new guy around my circle of friends this early in connecting with someone, but this was a special circumstance due to timing. I made Chad aware there were many single women in my friend group who would be at the fundraiser that were actively doing online dating. It was quite possible he would know some of these women since they were in the same age range as him.

The venue was beautifully decorated. The auction items lined several walls of the room, and they had a faux betting table set up too. On the far end of the room, they had a cash bar, and throughout the room, they had high-top table tables for people to hang out. The turnout for the event was impressive, and people kept coming up to me to say hello.

We roamed around the event and participated in the various auctions, in addition to the games, to help raise money for the cause.

Three of my girlfriends approached me in the first thirty minutes I was there. They each questioned my status with Chad, which I fully anticipated. They all informed me they were or had been in communication with Chad. One of those friends said, "I chatted with Chad earlier today, and we were making plans to go out next week."

Geez! I smiled at her and replied, "We have only been on a couple of dates thus far, we are not exclusive, and we don't owe each other anything at this point in the relationship."

I figured this could happen with so many single ladies at the same event. This is why I gave Chad a heads-up. We weren't exclusive, and we understood we were both dating other people concurrently.

Our first date, a week prior to the fundraiser, was at a local pub for happy hour. We had a lot of common interests, and I enjoyed our time together. Chad wanted to meet for dinner that Saturday, but I had the fundraiser to attend, which I could not miss. I suggested, "We could go to dinner and then go to the fundraiser together if you are interested?" I didn't want to assume he was interested in going to the fundraiser, but fortunately, he was, and we ended up having a marvelous time. That is where this "not so pretty" story began.

After the fundraiser, Chad walked me to my car and told me he had a very nice time. He asked me out the following week, and I happily accepted a third date with him.

He said he would make the plan and let me know the details shortly. As promised, Chad called me a couple of days later with the details of our date. I would meet him at his house, and we would go to dinner with his buddy and his wife. He said he was working on the plan for after dinner, which left me wondering what exactly he had in mind.

On the evening of the date, I headed out to his place. I gave myself extra time to get there since I had never been there before and was unfamiliar with the area. I ended up getting a ticket on my way to his place. This was not a good way to start the evening. This might have been my intuition telling me I should turn around and go back home! In hindsight, it was!

I arrived at Chad's home about ten minutes early. His home was tucked back into the woods, off a country road in the middle of nowhere. It was a traditional ranch-style house with a Tudor look and really cute. There wasn't a house visible from where I stood. Chad greeted me at the front door and welcomed me into his home. The inside decorations looked good, considering it was a bachelor pad. It didn't scream tacky and out of style like so many single men's homes.

I said, "You have a beautiful home, and it is so tastefully decorated!" I have to admit when I go to a man's home, I assess how much work needs to be done and try to envision how it would look if I lived there. It's just a thing I do!

We had a quick drink at his place before heading out, and boy did I need that one after getting a ticket. We got in Chad's car and drove to the Mexican restaurant to meet his friends. The four of us sat down at a table and ordered up some margaritas. The conversation with the couple was quite enjoyable, and I felt very comfortable with them. That is when Chad enlightened me on the plan to go watch a high school basketball game after dinner.

No offense, but who wants to go to a high school basketball game on a third date? Not me! I was less than enthralled to spend the next two to three hours of my life in a stinky gym, watching a team I didn't care about.

After dinner, we made our way over to the high school to watch the basketball game, and I completely disengaged from the whole plan. I couldn't wait for it to be over so I could go home. We were headed back to his house when he suddenly pulled into this bar.

He said, "Let's go for one before we call it a night."

We sat down, ordered drinks, and made small talk. We really didn't have the opportunity to chat much due to the events of the evening. We stayed there for about forty-five minutes before heading back to his place around 11 p.m. I was getting tired at that point and wasn't looking forward to the drive home.

It seemed like it took forever driving down all the dark country roads to get back to his place. When we finally arrived, he said, "Can you come in for a few minutes?"

I really wanted to get going because it was late, but I also needed to use the restroom before my long journey home. I obliged, and we went into his house.

While he let his dog out, he said, "Can I interest you in a glass of wine?"

I said, "As tempting as that sounds, I'm going to have to pass because I have to drive home."

He looked disappointed, but it wasn't worth getting a DUI.

"You could have a glass of wine with me and cuddle for a few hours and leave around 2 or 3 a.m.," he said.

I declined his offer and said, "That is an interesting idea, but I don't feel comfortable leaving here in the middle of the night, especially when I am unfamiliar with the area." I knew if I stayed, he would want to fool around, and I wasn't at a place where I was comfortable with that option. I reiterated I needed to use the bathroom, and he showed me where it was.

When I walked back into the kitchen, Chad was standing there waiting for his dog. Chad came over to me, gave me a big hug, and a very nice kiss. I thanked him for a fun evening and proceeded to get my purse on the counter across the kitchen.

Chad said, "Hey Karen, I had fun tonight!"

I glanced back at Chad to reply, and I couldn't believe my eyes! He was standing there with his pants and underwear down around his ankles. He gave me a creepy smile, pointed to his wiener, and said, "Isn't he pretty? Do you want to get to know my friend better?"

What the hell just happened?

How did it go from a nice hug and kiss to pants on the ground? I smiled, tried to laugh it off, and said, "Wow! Nothing like being direct!" I told him it was late, and I had to get going because it would take me almost an hour to get home.

I couldn't even take him seriously with his pants around his ankles. Chad shuffled over to the couch, sat down, patted the spot next to him, raised his eyebrows, like Groucho Marx, and tried to entice me to join him.

I chuckled and said, "Maybe next time, Chad," and made my dash for the door. I got into my car while muttering to myself, *"Oh, my God, that was crazy!"* I was gone before he could shuffle his way to the door to stop me! I arrived home safely and laughed myself to sleep.

The next day I was at a movie with some friends, when I saw Chad on a date with another woman! I wonder if she thought "it was pretty"? I never talked to Chad again after our date, but I learned to always listen to my intuition when it came to dating. Intuition is God's gift to women, and there were too many occurrences that my intuition was spot on, and I didn't pay attention. No mas!

CHAPTER 17:

SECRET AGENDA GUY

It was Saturday night, and I had a date planned, but he canceled on me last minute like he had done two times before. He always had some sort of bullshit excuse. I was too good for him, so I deleted him from the app and blocked him on my phone to avoid being bothered by him again. I was frustrated by this last-minute development and decided to get my ass off the couch. I got myself prettied up and went out on my own.

I ended up at one of my favorite Italian restaurants, and I ordered a glass of wine. I sat there sipping my delicious cabernet, pondering on my day and the douche bag who canceled on me. I ordered the calamari, which is one of my favorites. I savored every bite and soaked up the spicy marinara sauce with the delicious crusty bread. I hated to waste a single drop of it.

While I gorged myself on calamari, a delightful-looking man walked in and sat at the opposite end of the bar. I assumed he was waiting for a date, a wife, or something. A hot guy like that couldn't possibly be alone at the same bar as me. I made eye contact with him several times and tried not to be too obvious. I kept trying to eye spy his finger to see if he was wearing a wedding ring. Not that wearing a wedding ring means anything nowadays.

I knew the bartender by name since I was a regular at this particular place and called her over. I asked her to do me a favor and look to see if the hot guy at the end of the bar was wearing a wedding ring.

She did a very discrete flyby and glanced in my direction, and mouth the word "no." There was a 50 percent chance he wasn't married!

I called her over again and said, "Will you let that handsome specimen at the end of the bar know I think he is hot?"

She grinned and agreed to share my thought with the fine gentleman. I watched her make her way down the end of the where she leaned over and passed my message along to him. He glanced in my direction and gave me a pleasing smile. He stood up, grabbed his drink, and came down to my end of the bar. He situated himself next to me and introduced himself as Chad. I shook his hand and introduced myself.

We got acquainted for the next several hours and enjoyed a couple of glasses of wine. He was comfortable to talk to, not to mention easy on the eyes. He was very complimentary and made me blush. At the end of the evening, we made plans to get together a couple of days later. We exchanged digits and began texting almost immediately. I felt like we had an amazing connection, not to mention we met in such a random manner.

We were inseparable for the next three weeks. We went to an art gallery showing, lunches, dinners, and a Halloween party. We hung at his condo a couple of evenings and spent the weekends at mine. The intimacy wasn't off the charts, but it was enjoyable. He seemed to enjoy the adult activities, but I wasn't sure if he ever had a happy ending. There are obvious signs, and none were apparent to me. I knew I was content with the stimulation I was getting.

The day after the Halloween party, I drove him back to his place, and he leaned over and gave a hug and a kiss. I got a strange feeling when he got out of the car. I asked him in a jovial way, "What are we doing next weekend?" That is where the long pause happened, and I didn't get an answer, only a strange look.

I felt like that would be the last weekend we would spend together. I wasn't sure what triggered this mindset, but my intuition was my superpower, and it was on high alert. *Red flag!*

We talked later that evening, and again I inquired about our plans for the following weekend. I got a very convoluted answer that caught me off guard. He informed me he had plans that weekend which he made long before he met me. He was traveling to Savannah with a "girl" friend of his. This was a very awkward moment. I found it hard to believe he forgot to mention this weekend trip, with another woman, in the last three weeks. *Red flag!*

The week leading up to the big trip, he was very strange and distant. He asked me to meet him for lunch the day he was heading out of town. I agreed and met him at a place by work. There was definitely a different vibe between us. I asked him some pointed questions about his trip, and he was very vague with his answers. He couldn't tell me what airline he was flying on or what time he departed. He only knew approximately what time his flight left and hadn't checked in yet. He was well-traveled, so the process of checking in for a flight wasn't foreign to him. *Red flag!* He could tell I was very suspicious about the details of this secret trip. We finished lunch, and I had to return to work. He gave me a lame hug and told me he'd text me later.

The entire weekend from Thursday to Sunday, he was emotionally MIA. I got a couple of token text messages likely sent when the "secret lady" was in the shower or using the restroom. There was nothing heartfelt or emotional in his messages. They were just obligatory. *Red flag!* I decided I wasn't going to respond to his messages during the weekend. If he couldn't make me feel good, then don't make me feel insignificant either. Coincidently, I got a barrage of text messages on Sunday morning out of the blue. I am guessing the "secret lady" took another flight home, and now he was at the airport by himself. Suddenly he was free to communicate, and I was getting full grammatical sentences from him, versus the one or two-word messages I received all weekend.

I experienced this behavior in a past relationship, so this wasn't my first rodeo. Did he think I was stupid or naive? I ignored all of his messages for the remainder of the day. On Monday, I sent him an email spelling out my feelings and letting him know I didn't appreciate his secret weekend shenanigans or deceptive behavior. I ended it with Chad.

If things don't add up, and I don't know where I stand with someone, I will simply walk away and never look back!

CHAPTER 18:

THE POTHEAD

I met this guy recently, and his story is a perfect example of how I try to keep an open mind while dating. His name was Chad, and he was far from what I considered my "typical" guy. He was in good shape, talked with a twang, had multiple tattoos, a trimmed beard, and was rough around the edges. He worked in construction and wore Wrangler jeans to work. He didn't have a clue what a fancy restaurant was and rarely ate out.

I am not sure why I was drawn to him, but I was.

In the first ten minutes of our first date, I knew he wasn't for me and wanted to go home. I had no intention of going out with him again. He wasn't very cultured or fashionable and certainly wasn't well-traveled, but there was something about him I liked. I tried not to be shallow and keep an open mind since this was my "new" motto of dating. I decided to give him another shot and assumed his odd behavior was due to nerves. I was clearly out of his league.

Our second date happened on Sweetest Day, and we planned to visit some nurseries in search of a couple of new trees for my yard. We met at a mutual location and went in his truck from there. When I opened the door to his truck, I saw a beautiful wood crate filled with flowers and all kinds of goodies. He looked at me and said, "Happy Sweetest Day, Honey!"

I felt bad because this was only our second date, and I didn't feel obligated to get him any gifts at that point. I thanked him for his generous gifts and put the crate in my car. I got back in his truck, and we headed for the gas station.

Chad pulled up to the pump and jumped out of the truck. He attempted to pump gas, but it seemed like it took a long time. Abruptly, he got back in the truck, took a deep breath, covered his face with his hands, and said, "I am so fucking stoned!" That explained his inability to pump gas. He was finally successful on his third attempt.

I was pretty irritated he was stoned. I thought to myself, "He's f'g stoned? What the hell! He's putting my life at risk by driving this way." *Red flag!* I asked him, "Did you think it was a good idea to get stoned for our date?"

He looked at me and said, "I'm sorry, man!" This date qualified as his second chance, and it didn't seem promising. In hindsight, I should have made him take me back to my car and ended it there, but I didn't.

We visited some nurseries, found a couple of trees for my yard, and stopped for lunch on our way back to my car. Chad wasn't stoned anymore and was actually pleasant to talk to. We had a very enjoyable lunch and got to know each other a bit better. After lunch, he dropped me off at my car, and I thanked him again for the gifts.

We went to a fish fry the following weekend, followed by a two-hour tour around town to all the construction projects he had completed in the last five years. He told me how excited he was to tell his buddies about "his new girl" and how he thanked the Lord for putting me in his life. He said,

"I have never met anyone like you before and can't wait to see where this goes." He asked, "Can I call you, *my girl?*"

I wasn't sure what "*my girl*" meant and replied, "Your girl, like girlfriend?" My feelings weren't progressing in that direction with Chad.

When I talked to Chad on the phone over the next week, I detected something peculiar. He was hard to understand, slurred his words, and seemed drunk. I called him out for being sloshed on the phone. He admitted getting stoned and having several beers every night when he got home from work. This was certainly not an endearing quality I looked for in my person. He stopped taking my calls past 6 p.m. after that night. *Red flag!*

I realized Chad never ordered a drink when we went out yet got hammered every night at home, so I questioned him on it. Chad explained he got two DUIs in a five-year period and actually did some jail time for it. *Red flag!* That made perfect sense as to why he never drank when we were out. Why was I still talking to this guy? He was so not my type. I wanted to break it off, but Chad kept asking what I wanted for my birthday. I told him not to get me anything, and he said, "At least let me take you out for dinner." He told me to pick a place since he didn't have a clue about nice restaurants.

We ended up going to one of my favorite places for my birthday and having a really nice dinner, but I still wasn't feeling it for Chad. When dinner was over, he walked me to my car, and suddenly stopped and said, "Wait here." He ran to his car and returned with a box.

I said, "I told you not to get me anything."

He said, "It's a cake for your birthday!"

I thanked him for the cake and put it in my car. I think he expected me to invite him back to my house for cake, but that wasn't going to happen.

I got home and shared a piece of the cake with my daughter. Chad texted me several days later and asked if everything was okay because I had been very distant. It wasn't my plan to hurt him, but I had to end it. I put together a nice, heartfelt text, which explained how *I wasn't feeling it* with him and couldn't see him anymore. I told him I thought he was a great guy, and I hoped we could remain friends.

His initial response was normal, and he was sorry to learn he "wasn't my guy."

A couple of hours later, when he was stoned and drunk, he proceeded to text me very nasty things. He said he couldn't be friends with someone who turned their back on him. He told me I used him for "entertainment"! The final text included the song "What You Had" by Stevie Nicks. *Red flag!* Adios, Chad!

CHAPTER 19:

THE SINGING UNCLE

"Do you remember me?" my date asked.

He was tall, handsome, bald, had a great smile, and had an athletic build. He definitely looked familiar, but I couldn't place where I met him. Chad explained the car wash encounter several years prior, and I suddenly remembered him. He was the cute guy from the car wash who said, "You are absolutely beautiful and have amazing eyes." This was an interesting twist.

Chad and I continued to get acquainted and ordered some drinks. I ordered a blackberry margarita, and he got water. I looked at him and said, "Water?"

He explained he was seeing a shaman and was off alcohol for forty-eight days.

I said, "Really? What is a shaman?"

He explained a shaman helps you get your life and body in harmony. To do this, you can't drink, smoke, do drugs, and must meditate, in addition to consuming this special drink mixture throughout the day.

Chad paid him $1,500 a month for all of this BS knowledge! Can you say, "Sucker"? *Red flag!* I told him to pay me $1,000 a month, and I would tell him what to do!

Chad told me he frequented the bar we were at because his Uncle Bob lived nearby. Coincidently, Chad's phone rang, and it was the uncle. Ten minutes later, this attractive older man standing next to me says, "Hello there, hottie!"

Chad said, "Hi Uncle Bob, this is my date, Karen." Chad invited his uncle to join us on our first date, how lovely. Anything goes! I guess! I don't know who was more smitten, Chad or his uncle. I think his old uncle wanted to get to know me more than Chad.

We all talked about online dating and how crazy it is. Somehow the word yellow came into our discussion, and out of nowhere, the uncle broke out into song and started singing a couple of lines from "Tie a Yellow Ribbon…."! It caught me off guard but was hilarious. He continued this singing thing every time he heard a magic word that set him off into song. The uncle thought he was an amazing singer and loved the attention people gave him. It was funny the first five times, but after that, it got old really fast. The people sitting around us got annoyed too, and the looks on their faces showed it. The uncle picked up the tab at the end of the date, and we all went on our separate ways.

Chad and I went out about five more times over the next couple of weeks. One of those outings was to the driving range, and ironically, the singing uncle showed up mid-date. We went to a couple of happy hours, and again the singing uncle showed up. I thought it was incredibly odd that the singing uncle always surfaced on our dates. Each time the uncle showed up, a musical broke out. *Red flag!* The only "alone" dates we went on were at the VFW, where the drinks were dirt cheap. This was the day I decided I was done with this charade.

We had only had one date where it was just Chad and I.

Chad made comments like, "When are we going to get naked?" or "Let's go to your house for some fun." He would always find a way to brush his hand against my breast or butt. I wasn't anywhere close to being intimate with Chad. I felt like he was more interested in getting me in the sack than building a relationship. He hadn't even taken me out for a nice dinner yet, or a real date for that matter. Every date had been cheap eats and drinks, and the uncle usually paid. *Red flag!* This guy was not for me!

CHAPTER 20:

HOLY MOTHER OF PEARL

———

I noticed something strange on the toilet seat while using the guest bathroom. It looked like a string of poop was on the toilet seat. The last person to use this bathroom was Chad. Did he shit on the seat and leave it? How could you not notice such a thing and not clean up after yourself? So many questions went through my head. I wadded up some toilet paper and tried to wipe the said stuff off the seat. I realized it had hardened on and wouldn't come off. I took a bunch of Lysol wipes and piled them on top of the mess in hopes it would soften up and cleanup without issue.

I came back many hours later to clean up the seat. I grabbed the pile of wipes and wiped the spot. It didn't budge. It was still just as stuck on as it was hours before. What the hell! I scrubbed it a little and then started to laugh. I realized there was no poop on the seat, but instead, the seat had cracked and broken. Later, when I called Chad, I asked him if he noticed anything strange about the toilet seat, in the guest bathroom?

He said he noticed it was broken, and when he sat down on the seat, his ass got pinched in the crack. "Holy Mother of Pearl, that hurt," he said. He didn't know if he broke the seat or if it was already broken.

I laughed it off and told him my version of what I thought "it" was on the toilet seat until I realized it was just a crack. I was headed to Home Depot and told him I would get a new one, but he had to help me install it. He chuckled and told me he had already picked one up for me and not to worry. We laughed about that story for days, and I still laugh about this story to this day when I think about it!

We had plans to go to a friend's birthday party that weekend. Chad picked me up, and I could immediately tell something was off with him. His demeanor was different, he wouldn't hold my hand, and he was totally disengaged. Something had happened, and I didn't know what. The entire evening felt awkward, and it put a damper on my mood. I wasn't able to enjoy the festivities because I was so preoccupied trying to figure out what was going on with Chad. There was one point I thought of getting an Uber and just heading home without him.

On the car ride home, I asked, "You seem very off tonight, is everything okay? Is something bothering you? Have I done something to piss you off?"

He responded, "Everything is fine. You haven't done anything wrong. I just have a lot on my mind with the deal I am working on." I accepted that answer, but my intuition told me he wasn't being honest. *Red flag!* We got back to my house, and I assumed he was going to stay the night, but he abruptly left and said, "I have an early meeting tomorrow, so I am going to head home!" I knew without a doubt that something deeper was going on.

A couple of days later, I got a "Dear Karen" email from him. Yes, an email! He explained how he ran into his ex-girlfriend a couple of days earlier and realized he still had feelings for her. He admitted he wasn't over her and wasn't ready for a relationship with me. He expounded on the fact he didn't have a job, lived in an extended stay hotel, and claimed to have no money. He asked me to give him three months to get his shit together. I was sad and hurt because I really liked him.

I wasn't going to put my life on hold for three months and wait for something that may never happen. I pulled up my big girl pants and decided to forge on in the dating world once again. My stint with Chad was amazing but short-lived and ended after three marvelous weeks.

It was only a couple of weeks later I met a nice guy and started dating him. Three months to the day, Chad called. I was on my way to work and completely thrown off when I saw his call come across my phone. I did a triple take to make sure I saw it correctly. I answered his call and had a nice high-level conversation with him. Shortly after our call, he messaged me and told me how nice it was to hear my voice again. He asked, "Would you be interested in meeting me for a drink and start over as friends?" I was in a relationship for almost three months at that point, so I didn't feel comfortable meeting him.

We recently met for that drink as friends. Chad wanted to explain the events that led to the "Dear Karen" email, and he apologized for how things went down.

Let's rewind to how I met Chad.

I was at my wit's end with dating and was ready to delete all of my accounts and give up on dating forever when I got a "like" from a guy named Chad. I checked out his pictures and profile, and he seemed decent. I "liked" him back, and we started to chat. I was feeling very spontaneous and suggested we meet the next day.

He was all for it!

I got to the restaurant a couple of minutes early and ordered myself a glass of wine. Chad arrived, and I thought he was a lot more attractive in person than he was in his pictures. Chad was about 6,' handsome face, stunning eyes, a thick head of wavy hair, nice build, and dressed well. I was pleasantly surprised, and we really hit it off from the start. The date felt like it lasted ten minutes, but it was actually four hours long. I couldn't believe it. This kind of thing rarely happened to me. He kissed me goodnight at my car, and it was magical. He was an amazing kisser, and I could have kissed him for hours.

The next two weeks, we spent a lot of time together, and I loved every second of it. He made my heart happy, and I could see him in my future. Our personalities jived, and he made me laugh like not many have. He said "Holy Mother of Pearl" no less than twenty times a day. It was his signature response, and it cracked me up every time he said it! There was something magical about him that made me glow and smile like few men had.

Chad took me out to a nice dinner at my favorite local steak house. We made our way back to my house for a nightcap at the end of the evening, and one thing led to another. The intimacy between us that night was exceptional, and I fell asleep grinning from ear to ear.

This story is a good example of when I should have listened to my intuition!

PART 4:

TOO CHEAP
TO KEEP

CHAPTER 21:

ALLIGATOR ARMS

"Really? Is that a bad thing?" Chad said.

I responded, "Well, it isn't a good thing, I can tell you that!" This ended up being one of two times in all of my dating adventures, I picked up the entire tab on a date. There was a giant *red flag* with Chad, and he was too cheap to keep!

Chad was about 5' 9," extremely fit, and had a smoking hot body. He had an arrogance about himself that was over the top. I met Chad at a downtown wine bar, and there was chemistry between us right out of the gate. The conversation was well balanced, though it was obvious Chad loved talking about himself. Thank goodness he was easy on the eyes, or it might have become an unpleasant situation.

I am all about a good happy hour, so I typically offer that option for a first or second date. We had a couple of glasses of happy hour wine and appetizers. The company, conversation, and food were all good. This was a successful date in my mind, and I hoped Chad was interested in going out again. Our date was coming to an end when this girl walked over to us and started talking nonstop. This chatty woman was Chad's ex-girlfriend, and he didn't seem phased by her presence.

This ex-girlfriend yammered on and on. She inquired where I worked, lived, and how many kids I had. It felt weird that Chad's ex, a total stranger, was interrogating me. She told me all about her role at a local life insurance company. I gave her my business card and told her to call me. I hoped this would be her clue to remove herself from our date.

When the check came, I handed Chad some money to cover half of the cost. Chad declined my monetary offer and graciously paid the bill. I made it a practice to always offer my date some money and contribute to the bill. Chad and I stood up and started making our way to the door. It was undisputed we enjoyed our time, and we both acknowledged we would like to see each other again. We set a time for the following week to meet.

It seemed like I blinked, and I was meeting Chad again, which I was excited about. We arrived for our second date in a punctual fashion at a location not far from our first rendezvous. Our date played out similar to the first, with good conversation, complemented with happy hour drinks and appetizers. This made for a great second date, or so I thought.

Chad spent a good portion of our second date talking about how much he loved to work out every part of his body. I was thoroughly impressed by his incredibly toned body, but it got old hearing about how great he thought he was for the entirety of our date. I tried to interject some details about myself, but I got shut down, and the conversation reverted right back to Chad.

The date came to an end, after about three hours, which indicated another successful date. Chad looked across the bar, made eye contact with the server, and motioned for the check. The server presented us with the bill right away, but it sat there in front of us for the next forty-five minutes while we continued to talk. Chad made no attempt to pay for the bill, look at the bill, acknowledge the bill, or reach for his wallet. This perplexed me since he was so quick to pick up the tab on our first date. It's not that I expected him to pay the entire bill again, but he seemed oblivious the check existed.

I made the first move and grabbed the check to review it. I said, "Let's see what damage we did today." I perused the item level detail of the bill and reached into my purse for my wallet. I fully expected to pay my portion, but Chad still hadn't acknowledged the bill in front of him and made no attempt to initiate payment.

I proceeded to get out my credit card and put it on the bar in front of me. "I figured I'd let you get the bill this time since I got it on our last date," Chad said. *Red flag!*

I chuckled and said, "Oh really? Okay then, I guess I will pay the bill." I was irritated by this, and Chad could tell. As a rule, I always offer to pay my portion of the tab, but expecting me to pay the whole thing, and on a second date?

In my opinion, a true gentleman wouldn't allow a woman to pay the whole tab within the first few months of dating. Once established in a relationship with someone, I am totally comfortable picking up the tab on a regular basis and sharing expenses accordingly.

CHAPTER 22:

HANKY MAN

———

The meal and conversation with Chad were enjoyable as usual, but every five minutes, Chad reached into his pants pocket and pulled out a handkerchief to blow or dig out his nose. Yes, I said a handkerchief! *Red flag!* He would dig his hankie finger so deep into his nose it made my nose hurt. Only men older than seventy years old are grandfathered into this generational privilege to use a hanky. What fifty-year-old man uses a hanky and on a date? The thought of my date wiping his boogers on a piece of material and then putting it back in their pocket over and over again is just plain gross.

Let me start from the beginning.

It was that time of year for our annual "18-Hole Hooky Golf Day" at my friend's country club. I was really excited to wear the new golf outfit I bought for the occasion. We had a blast like usual, and the day was filled with lots of laughter and fun conversation.

My friend's house is on the eleventh hole, and we stopped there to do our token Fireball shot. We planted ourselves on four barstools in the clubhouse bar, after the round, for our customary post-golf libation.

An extremely handsome man came in and sat down catty-corner from me at the bar. The first order of business was to look for a wedding band on his left hand, and there wasn't one. This was promising, but I reminded myself "no ring" didn't necessarily mean he wasn't married. I made my introduction and shook his hand.

His name was Chad, and he was very good-looking. He was around 6'5", athletic build, in good shape, well-manicured, striking blue eyes, balding on the crown of his head, and a well-groomed beard. I am typically not a fan of facial hair on my guys, but Chad's beard suited him nicely.

He was wearing a Michigan State sweatshirt, which happened to be my alma mater's rival school. This made it easy to start a dialogue and learn more about him. I looked at him and said, "I went to Central Michigan. Did you go to Michigan State?" He confirmed he went to Michigan State, and I said, "Fire Up Chips!" He smiled because he knew what that meant.

I gave him my high-level explanation of why I had golfed at Fox Meadow that day. I told him how beautiful the houses were on the golf course. He told me he lived on the ninth hole. I asked, "How long have you and your wife lived here?" He said he was divorced, lived with his son, and was at the clubhouse that evening to pick up his take-out order.

The conversation went well, and we had a lot in common. We reminisced about our college days and the rivalry between our two schools. I felt very comfortable talking with him, and it felt like I had known him longer than an hour. Chad's son came in at one point to inquire about the status of their take-out order. Chad handed his son the to-go bags, the key to the golf cart, and told him to start dinner without him. He assured his son he wouldn't be too far behind him.

My girlfriends left, and I stayed behind to continue chatting with Chad. This kind of connection and comfort level was a rare occurrence for me. We talked for another hour before I decided to head home. Chad walked me to my car and gave me the most amazing kiss. We made plans to see each other again in a couple of days. While standing there, it dawned on me his son took his golf cart, and he had to walk home. I offered him a ride to his house, and he graciously accepted.

I pulled into his driveway and complimented him on his beautiful home. I told him what a pleasure it was to meet him, and he concurred. He leaned over, and we proceeded to have a wonderful make out session. We said our goodbyes, and I went on my way. I was elated by what had transpired with Chad.

I was ten minutes into my drive home when my phone rang. Chad called me, and he wanted to alert me to a road closure. We talked the entire way home, and then for another hour once I got home. I am not a huge phone talker, so it was unheard of for me to spend this much time talking to someone.

Sweetest Day is a made-up holiday for lovers and was four days away. Chad wanted to take me to dinner. I was super excited to see Chad again and couldn't remember the last time I felt so eager to see someone. We spent a lot of time talking on the phone over the next four days. It all seemed too good to be true.

Sweetest Day arrived, and I was elated to see Chad. I pulled into his driveway and let him know I had arrived. He opened the garage door and told me to come in. I envisioned what the inside of his house would look like and was anxious to see it.

He opened the door, greeted me with a big smile, and brought me into the kitchen. He welcomed me with one of his incredible kisses. He said, "Wait here, I have a surprise for you." He disappeared down the basement stairs, and I stood there checking out his place.

His house was absolutely stunning and well-manicured from the outside, but the inside left something to be desired. It was totally different from what I visualized. Everything was outdated and screamed "*extreme makeover needed.*"

Chad emerged from the basement holding a small bouquet of brown, half-dead roses. He said, "The Lion's Club was selling these at the traffic light on the corner." *Huh?* The polite me pretended to like the flowers and the gesture, but the inner me was thinking, "*What the hell!*" *Red flag!*

I know it's the thought that counts, but who gives half-dead flowers to a woman they're interested in? Was this supposed to impress me? Regardless of how I felt, I thanked him for the roses and acted delighted.

He gave me a tour of his house, and I became less impressed the more I saw. The carpet had pet issues, the furniture looked thirty years old, every TV was the old box type, the brown-orange color scheme was horribly drab, and I felt like I flashed back into the 1980s. This house turned out to be such a disappointment on the inside and definitely didn't have a woman's touch

His bedroom had a waterbed. Who has a waterbed anymore? Red flag!

I don't know why that surprised me, based on the decor in the rest of his house. Once the tour was done, we headed out to dinner.

We went to a steak place where you cook your own steak on a hot stone. The concept is cool, but if I wanted to cook my own meal, I would have stayed home and cooked. Ironically, there wasn't a price cut on my meal for self-cooking it. I would rather have the restaurant prepare the steak for the same price. I wasn't paying, so I guess it really didn't matter.

Over the next couple of weeks, I got to know Chad more. The more I learned about him, the more disenchanted I became. I found out some things that made me really ponder. He had never taken a vacation and didn't plan to until he retired. He had been saving for that day to come. I couldn't believe it! I said, "I require at least one vacation a year, and that is nonnegotiable. What if something happened, and you never made it to retirement? You would have saved all that money for naught." Chad didn't have a response to my question and stood strong on his vacation theory. This was a giant *red flag* for me. I couldn't be with someone who didn't want to travel until retirement. A partner who likes to travel is a quality I demand.

This was just crazy. The *red flags* started piling up, and the *"Karen snowball"* started its descent. It was the beginning of the end for Chad.

I met Chad after work for a drink to break up with him. I positioned myself at a table, so I could see when Chad had arrived. He was smiling from ear to ear as he walked into the restaurant. He was oblivious about the hammer I was about to drop. He greeted me at the table with a kiss and a hug.

We started with some basic small talk. I didn't beat around the bush and got right down to business. I told him I thought he was a great guy but felt I had different expectations for a potential life partner. I referenced the *red flags* that became apparent to me. I told him I didn't see this working out for us.

Chad was so very sad, and he didn't see this coming at all! I said, "I am so sorry that our story didn't have a better ending." I got up, gave him a hug, and left.

PART 5:

THE FOREVER FRIEND ZONE

CHAPTER 23:

THE SKI ADDICT

———

It was my groundhog's day of dating, and it repeated itself at least once a year for ten years.

Chad was a tall, good-looking pharmacist. He had a great smile, striking features, great personality, drank wine, golfed, biked, skied, and loved to travel. Every time I entered the dating scene, Chad's profile would surface, and we would both "like" each other. The "dating dance" would play out the same way with texting, chatting, and planning a date. Several dates would happen before one or both of us became inattentive or disengaged, and "we" would fade off into the sunset.

Chad was an avid skier who was rarely home between November and May because he traveled out west. Every time we got traction dating, the disconnect happened because he was gone skiing. Sometimes he was gone for just a weekend, and other times weeks at a time. It was difficult to grow a relationship with someone who wasn't around. If he was truly interested in pursuing a relationship, he would make more of an effort and not go dark for long periods of time. There was definitely a connection between us, but I firmly believed if it was to happen, it would. It never did, or not yet at least.

We talked about the impending skiing season on one of our dates. He said, "Why don't you come with me to Colorado on one of my trips?"

I was open to going with him on a skiing adventure but wasn't overly committal since I didn't know if I would be dating someone when the time came. I knew the trip would be expensive, so not being able to afford it would be my excuse if I needed one. I told him, "I am interested, but I will have to see where I am financially when the time comes."

Chad had so many miles from all his trips he offered to use his flier miles for my flight. He explained he would get a hotel room and a rental car regardless of if I joined him or not. Me going to Colorado had no impact on his planning details. He assured me there would be two queen beds in our hotel room, seeing as though we had never done more than a little kissing. This idea seemed a little awkward at first, but I figured I would be able to manage. I was responsible for a couple lift tickets, and that was basically all. Chad would pick up the cost of my ski rentals and one of my lift tickets as well. It was an enticing offer, which would be difficult to turn down.

Decision time came, and I had to agree to go or decline the offer to join him skiing. I accepted his invitation and was very excited yet a little apprehensive at the same time. Chad was always a gentleman on our dates, so I wasn't worried about that. He wouldn't overstep his boundaries unless it was consensual. This was a great opportunity to determine the potential of this relationship.

The trip was upon us, and we met at the airport. The flight was uneventful, and there wasn't the slightest bit of closeness between Chad and me. I put my hand on his leg to gauge his interest in us. He put his hand on top of mine, but it was difficult to get a read on his position with us. *Red flag!* We arrived in Denver, gathered our bags, and made our way to the rental car desk. In no time we were off, and on our way. It was supposed to be a two–three-hour drive to our hotel, where we stayed that night. Between the weather and traffic, the drive ended up being four hours. We were pretty wiped out by the time we arrived at the hotel. Chad checked in, and we made our way to our room. As promised, there were two beds in the room, and I felt totally comfortable with the sleeping arrangements.

We got cleaned up and decided, since the weather was mild, to walk into town to get some dinner. I held his hand as we made our way to the restaurant. He seemed unmoved by the gesture I initiated. We stumbled upon a charming Italian restaurant where we had a very nice dinner which included a delicious bottle of wine. We stopped for a nightcap at a cute little pub on our way back to the hotel, where we discovered Palomas, which became our drink of choice during the trip. Chad picked up the tab for everything that evening. We made our way back to the hotel, crawled into our designated beds, and fell asleep in less than ten minutes.

We were up and on our way early the next morning. We stopped to get some breakfast and headed to pick up my ski rentals. The hour in the car was very relaxed and laid-back. We had great conversation, about many topics. We finally arrived at Copper Mountain and prepared for a day of skiing. It was a beautiful day. The sky was a beautiful blue color, and the air was very crisp. We skied twenty miles the first day, and my legs felt like rubber bands.

We made our way to this beautiful hotel that would be our accommodation for the next two nights. We got settled into our room and were content to see two beds. We opened a bottle of wine and made our way to the hot tub, where I soaked my sore legs. We finished the bottle and headed back to the room to get ready for dinner.

Chad made a reservation at a swanky place. The food was delicious, and we had a very nice evening. Chad picked up the tab for our dinner and would not let me pay. We were having a nightcap, at the bar when the man to my left blatantly hit on me. He extended some complimentary remarks, and Chad was not happy. I had never seen this side of Chad before but was relieved to see some type of reaction from him after all this time. He acted like my boyfriend in all aspects, except for closeness or intimacy. I made many small advances on several occasions and got no response or reciprocation from him.

The next couple of days included many miles of skiing. The weather remained gorgeous, and I relished being in such a beautiful place, doing something I loved. The trip was coming to an end, and we were headed home soon. We had a couple more delightful dinners accompanied by more great conversation. Chad had not attempted to make a single move on me, even when I allowed him to sleep in the same bed with me one night. I knew we were both exhausted from skiing, but he fell asleep in record time, and there was absolutely no cuddling or touching whatsoever. I didn't know if I should feel flattered or insulted.

We stopped for lunch at the top of the mountain on our last day of skiing. We were taking in all the splendor of our surroundings when he said, "I had this strange dream about us last night! You and I were having crazy, wild sex."

I said, "It's probably because it's the elephant in the room!"

He questioned, "What does that mean?"

I explained, "Over the last ten years, our relationship has never progressed past kissing and has been on and off.

I didn't know what the expectation of sex would be on this trip." I told him I was open to sex, but didn't want it to ruin our friendship, especially if we would be staying in the friend zone. I wasn't sure he understood my position on the whole topic, but he nodded like he did.

We skied down to the bottom of the mountain, where he turned and looked at me and said, "Did you smell something bad?"

I said, "No, I didn't."

He laughed and said, "That's good because I was farting the entire way down!"

I chuckled and made some silly comment. I think Chad considered me "one of the guys." Quite frankly, I learned more about his bodily habits than I would like to admit. I thought Chad would have been more cognizant of his bathroom habits, and bodily noises, on our maiden voyage together. Red flag!

We made our way back to a hotel close to the airport the next day. Chad made a last-minute decision to head to Utah for a couple of more days of skiing, which I was indifferent about. My flight was at eleven the next morning, so I didn't have to wake up super early. Chad's flight was at 5 a.m., so he was up and out by 3:30 a.m. He kissed me on his way out and told me what a wonderful time he had with me. I was really caught off guard by this. Where was his desire to kiss me all week? I told him I had a wonderful time as well and thanked him for all his generosity. He sent me a text a couple of hours later letting me know he arrived in Utah.

I got home late that evening and prepared for work the next day. I didn't hear from Chad again for several weeks, and when I did, it was a token text. Chad fell into his normal nonstop skiing marathon, and it was late spring before

I heard from him again. I followed all his ski trips on social media, so I knew what he was up to. That is where history repeats itself, and we faded off into the sunset again.

Chad was undatable, and unless something changed, he would remain in the friend zone

CHAPTER 24:

SHAME ON ME

I can't believe I was a sucker for the same guy three times. It will never happen again, that's for sure. Fool me once, shame on me. Fool me twice, shame on you. Fool me three times, and strike you're out!

When I first started into this dating craziness, I met a stocky little man named Chad while at a happy hour with my friend from work? Chad was bald, wore little round glasses, was out of shape, not overly attractive, shorter than me, bald, and was a doctor. He wasn't the kind of guy I was typically attracted to, but I promised myself to keep an open mind when dating.

The night we met, he was with one of his doctor friends. The four of us sat at the bar had a marvelous time laughing and telling stories. I was very impressed when the little doctor picked up the entire tab at the end of the evening and asked me for my number.

Chad asked me out on a date a couple of days later, and I accepted. He took me out to a fabulous dinner at a very classy restaurant, where we feasted on a variety of dishes. The next day we played nine holes of golf, followed by another wonderful dinner, with great conversation. There was something about this little man I really liked, and he continued to grow on me. We went on several more dates over the next month, and there was never any pressure for sex or intimacy. The first strike occurred one evening when Chad and I had plans to go to dinner. He messaged me hours before he was supposed to pick me up and canceled our plans. He informed me about a funeral he had to attend and would call me later to reschedule our date. I told him I understood and gave him my condolences. I tried to be respectful of his situation, but after four days of not hearing from Chad, I reached out to him. I learned the funeral he attended was that of his ex-girlfriend's father. Chad realized, in consoling her, he still had feelings for her and wanted to give it another try. I was a little perturbed about the whole situation but accepted his story and gracefully walked away. That was that! *Red flag!*

The second strike played out three years later when I ran into Chad at the same place we originally met. He saw me and did a double take. Once again, he was with one of his buddies, and I was with a friend. He came over to where my friend and I sat once his colleague left. We all chatted for a bit, and my friend made her exit. Chad and I continued talking and catching up on life for the next couple of hours.

He informed me he was no longer with the *"funeral"* woman he dumped me for. I remained guarded but enjoyed his company. He asked. "Would you be interested in going to dinner with me?" I accepted his offer, and we made a plan for that weekend.

He picked me up that Friday in his fancy sports car and took me to an amazing restaurant on the eastside. He was the furthest thing from cheap and he spared no expense when it came to wining and dining. The evening felt really comfortable, and we picked up exactly where we left off three years before. There was something I really enjoyed about Chad, and I found myself falling for him again.

He was intelligent, funny, a bit self-important but had a tad too much drama in his life. We spent a lot of time together over the next month, and it played out very similar to our first go around. We still had never had sex or been intimate. I started to get a weird vibe from Chad, and it felt like the past was repeating itself. A week later, Chad went dark on me again just like he had before. I reached out to him to find out why he went MIA on me.

He responded in a timely manner and informed me he had developed feelings for a *"lady neighbor friend"* of his and wanted to pursue a relationship with her. He told me it wasn't until we started dating that the neighbor became interested in him. I gracefully departed from Chad again. I was pissed and felt like he had played me again. *Red flag!* What was with this guy? I wasn't going to let this happen again, or so I thought.

The third and final strike happened three years later, at the same venue the first two strikes began. I got to the restaurant early to get a spot at the bar for happy hour. I was confident in how particularly good I looked that night and had an extra skip in my step.

I made my way to the end of the bar and made eye contact with a man who was checking me out. It was Chad, the little doctor! He was with a colleague having a very deep conversation when he noticed me and grinned from ear to ear. He looked at me and said, "Hi, Karen."

I paused and replied, "It's Chad, right?" I knew it was him, but I played dumb.

We did the normal niceties, and he asked how I was doing? I gave him the three-year canned answer about my life and said, "Everything is rainbows and unicorns. You?" I patted him on the shoulder, expressed my pleasure of seeing him, and made my way to the two open seats at the end of the bar.

My friend Susan joined me, and we enjoyed some fine wine, dinner, and great conversation. Chad said goodbye to his colleague, and in a blink, he was standing next to me. He interjected himself into our conversation and asked if we were going to buy him a drink.

I replied, "We don't buy men drinks. They buy us drinks!"

He smiled and bought himself a drink. We hung out for about an hour and decided it was time to head out. Chad ended up picking up our entire tab for the evening. I felt like he owed me that after the bullshit he put me through over the years.

The next day, I got the predictable text from Chad asking me out to dinner. I wasn't as quick to accept this time and said I had to check my schedule. I wasn't sure I wanted to set myself up for his nonsense again. I discussed my dilemma with a couple of my close confidants. They both agreed I should at least have dinner with Chad and give him a chance to explain himself.

I contacted Chad and accepted his invitation to join him for dinner that Friday night. We went to this exquisite restaurant I had always wanted to try, and it totally lived up to its reputation. During dinner, we caught up on the last three years.

He ended up marrying the *"lady neighbor friend"* he dumped me for during *strike two* and divorced her two years later. I didn't feel sorry for him, to be honest. We went out a couple more times, and once again, I felt the same weird vibe coming from Chad. I knew how this was going to play out, and it did! I didn't feel a connection with Chad this time and knew it wouldn't progress past friendship. I wasn't going to be played just to be dumped again. I pulled back from Chad and was extremely unresponsive and distant. I am sure Chad sensed it. A week later, he called and let me know he wasn't ready to date anyone or be in a relationship. *Red flag!* He assured me he wasn't seeing anyone else and was very busy with work. He wanted to spend time with his kids and grandchildren, or so he said!

I laughed and accepted his bullshit reasoning. I vowed I would never allow myself to fall for this little doctor again. I was too good for him, and he didn't realize what he had when he had it. It was his loss and not mine. Hurt me once, shame on me. Hurt me twice, shame on you. Hurt me a third time, and you're just a loser.

CHAPTER 25:

NO PLAN MAN

I was in a good place in my life. I wasn't on any dating sites. I was enjoying life and learning how to love myself, because you can't truly love another until you know how to love yourself.

A dating hiatus means my life is relaxed and uncomplicated. Looking through a million profiles and responding to messages isn't part of my daily routine. My time and schedule belong exclusively to me.

Online dating can be a full-time job and exhausting.

It all began at a happy hour when one of my best friends told me about her upcoming Put-In-Bay weekend. PIB is an island on Lake Erie, set in a boating/marina setting, and has lots of bars, pools, restaurants, and it is only accessible by ferry. It is known for its party atmosphere, especially after dark. A limited number of cars are allowed on the island, so visitors get around via golf carts.

She asked me if I was interested in joining them and said I could stay in their hotel room.

I said, "Hell yes," and just like that I had plans for the weekend.

We met at the ferry dock, and in no time, we were off! We arrived at the island, picked up our golf cart, and checked into our hotel room. My friend and her husband would share one bed, while their friend Chad and I shared the other bed. I had never met Chad before, but I figured I could share a bed with just about anyone. It was just a place to sleep, right? We all showered and got beautiful after spending a fun-filled day at the pool. Once a year, for one week, mayflies cover every surface imaginable and are absolutely disgusting. We didn't realize it was mayfly season when the four of us made our way across this grassy field to our golf cart.

We found ourselves swallowed up in a swarm of these harmless mayflies. As meaningless as these mayflies may be, they are just plain nasty and freaked me out. They got caught in our hair and clothes, and we screamed like little girls as we ran to the golf cart! The key was to keep your mouth shut so you don't swallow any of these dreadful bugs. We laughed about this experience the entire weekend.

We met up with the rest of the group and grabbed some dinner. We ate dinner and made our way to the bar zone, where the fun continued into the night. It was a drunken night filled with fun and laughter.

Chad and I got to know each other over the course of two days, and the more I hung out with him, the more he grew on me. There was some mutual flirting going on, and I tried to be discreet about it. Chad and I got separated from the group at one point, and he said, "I want to kiss you!" The kiss turned into a five-minute make-out session, and I enjoyed it. We eventually caught up with the group and the evening of imbibing carried on until the wee hours of the morning.

We made our way back to the hotel and crawled into our designated sleeping spots. There was a lot of sexual tension between Chad and I, but in the end, sleep prevailed. There was some secret touching going on under the covers, unbeknownst to my friend and her husband.

Morning came, and I packed up to head home. I didn't want the fun to end but knew reality was right around the corner. In a blink, we were on the ferry and headed to the mainland. I reminisced about my fun weekend as I drove home. Chad and I exchanged our information and planned to get together the following week.

Chad and I managed to get together several times in the next month, despite his crazy travel schedule. He was always very generous and didn't exhibit signs of cheapness. My birthday was right around the corner, and Chad asked me, "What do you want to do for your birthday?"

I said, "Surprise me!"

The day of my birthday, Chad picked me up, and we made our way downtown to the Blue Point. We started with some oysters and escargot, followed by some lobster and a small filet, done medium-rare. Everything was delicious, and I enjoyed the company in addition to the conversation. My friend and her husband met up with us after dinner in the Foundation Room at The House of Blues to watch some band. Chad was a big music fanatic and knew every band that ever existed. The music was good, the company was better, and we had an outstanding time together.

Chad got me a beautiful Coach purse and a bottle of Bond #9 perfume for my birthday. I was gracious for the wonderful gifts and thanked Chad. He dropped me off at my house at the end of the evening and headed home.

I only saw Chad a couple of times in the next month due to his hectic travel schedule. We talked about our holiday plans the next time we met for dinner. Chad would be with his kids over the holidays and back in Ohio after that. He asked me what we were doing for New Year's Eve. I explained I would still be in Chicago with my family until after the new year.

Chad asked, "I'd like to come to Chicago and spend New Year's Eve with you?"

I said, "I would like that."

I told Chad to make sure he flew into O'Hare International Airport, twenty-five minutes from my sister's house. He understood and said he would make his flight arrangements into O'Hare and would let me know his itinerary.

I didn't think much more about it until a week before NYE, and I realized I didn't know Chad's itinerary. I asked, "What are your plans for NYE?" He emailed me his flight information and was irritated to learn he booked a flight into Midway Airport after I specifically told him not to. I called him immediately and said, "I told you not to book your flight into Midway because of logistics, and you did anyway." *Red flag!* He said he forgot but would look into another flight into O'Hare.

Chad called me back about an hour later and said, "There are no other reasonably priced flights into O'Hare Airport this late in the game. I will just keep my existing flight and get a rental car from Midway to your sister's house." That was an acceptable option to me.

New Year's Eve was upon here, and so was a horrible snowstorm that dropped six inches of snow on the ground by 10 a.m. that morning. Chad's flight was supposed to arrive at 3 p.m., but the weather report predicted an additional twelve inches of snow that day. Chad's flight landed without incident, but it took him three-plus hours to get to my sister's house.

The party was wonderful, and we awoke to an additional fifteen inches of snow on the ground. No one was going anywhere on New Year's Day. We all just hunkered down and watched movies all day long. Chad was very clingy all day and had to be touching me or next to me every single minute. Even my sister noticed his odd behavior and said, "What is with Chad? He has to be attached to you every moment?" I said, "Trust me, he's driving me crazy too." *Red flag!*

Later that day, my sister asked what the game plan was for the next couple of days. I explained we planned to spend the following night in Chicago to see the blues concert and return the following day when Chad would fly home.

As I explained these plans to my sister, Chad interrupted me and said, "I don't have a flight back to Cleveland yet!"

I was like, W*what?*" I said, "What do you mean you don't have a return flight back?"

He replied, "I thought I would just drive back with you."

I explained to him I wasn't going to have room in my car going back. I already had five people, a dog, and all of our shit to bring back to Cleveland. I was pissed he just assumed he could ride back with us. I said, "Wouldn't you check with me before presuming you could ride back with us?" *Red flag!* Chad was speechless and could tell I was annoyed by the itinerary he created.

I woke the next morning to the sound of a snowblower. I looked outside and saw my sister trying to clear her driveway, so she could go to work. My sister has MS, so the thought of her trying to handle a snowblower scared me. I didn't want her to slip and fall.

I jumped out of bed, threw on some clothes, and headed outside to help my sister. Chad woke up and asked me what I was doing.

I replied, "I need to help my sister clear the driveway because it snowed twelve inches last night." I finished clearing the driveway for my sister, and she left for work. Chad walked outside right when I was putting the snowblower away, wearing a thin leather coat, fancy loafers with no socks and no hat or gloves. Did he really come to Chicago in the middle of winter without a hat or gloves?

I went back inside and warmed up from the frigid weather. We prepared to leave for the train station, and I asked, "Did you bring a hat, gloves, or a heavier coat?" I said, "You do realize you are in Chicago in the winter, right? Your feet are going to freeze in those little loafers."

He shrugged his shoulders at me and said, "Oh well!" *Red flag!*

We finally arrived in the city and made our way to the taxi stand. We jumped in a cab and zipped over to our hotel. During the cab ride, Chad leaned over and whispered in my ear, "We should take a nap when we get checked into our room."

A nap? Who goes down to Chicago to take a nap?

I said, "Really, a nap? We are in Chicago, you know?"

He quickly retracted that suggestion and never mentioned it again.

Chad and I had never been intimate in the four months we dated. This overnight getaway in Chicago was our first opportunity to spend the entire night together *alone*. Not that the thought of sex never crossed our minds, but the timing never worked out.

Chad went up to the front desk to check in, and I sat down on a nearby couch. It seemed like it was taking a long time. Chad made his way over to me, and I asked him, "What took so long?"

He replied in a soft tone, "I screwed up! I made reservations for tomorrow, not today!" The blues concert and hotel reservation were both for the following night! We were a day early. *Red flag!*

He booked another room for that night since we were already down in the city. I wasn't upset about the blues concert part because I didn't know who the musician was anyway. It looked at Chad and said, "It looks like it's going to be a bar crawl kind of day in Chicago." We went up to the room to drop off our bags and headed for lunch!

The bar crawl ended up being a lot of fun. We spent the day imbibing around the city and hit a lot of fun places for yummy eats along the way. Chad loved bourbon, so we managed to find several hot spots with these specialized spirits.

It was midnight when we headed back to the hotel. I hoped there would be some adult activities, considering this was our first "alone" sleepover. Unfortunately, the whiskey won, and Chad fell asleep within ten minutes of hitting the pillow. *Red flag!* Clearly, I didn't get the loving I had hoped for, and I was very disappointed. I couldn't understand why he thought it would be a good idea to go overboard on bourbon when he knew this would be our *first time*. Even if he hadn't fallen asleep, we would have contended with the infamous "whiskey dick" struggle. I had a buzz, but nothing crazy. I wanted the sex I waited four months to have.

He woke up in the morning and wanted *morning sex*. He snuggled up close to me with his "morning missile" and tried to get frisky. I wasn't having that! Last night's nonevent still ticked me off. I didn't want our first time to include morning breath, pillow head, and overnight makeup face.

I told him I wasn't interested in sex and scolded him for drinking so much bourbon he passed out. I said, "You knew last night was our first chance to have sex since we met each other. I am not sure why you felt the need to drink yourself into oblivion?"

He said nothing, got up, and went into the bathroom to shower.

We stopped at Shaw's Crab House for some delicious oysters on our way to the train station. I am not sure if there is any truth to it, but some people believe oysters make you horny. I was already horny without the oysters.

I tried to swallow one of the larger oysters, but my gag reflex was having nothing to do it, and it launched right out of my mouth onto the plate. Plop, there it is!

Chad looked at me and said, "What the heck just happened?" Ugh, I tried it again, and "plop" out it came again! I made one last attempt at this oyster to no avail. That damn oyster plopped right out of my mouth. No sooner did it hit my plate Chad stabbed it with his fork and gobbled it up! *Red flag!*

We made our way to the train station, and in no time, we were headed back to my sister's house. Chad knew I had to get packed up, so we could leave the next morning. Chad recognized how much I had to do and didn't want to hinder my progress, so he decided to leave once we got back. I was relieved because I didn't need a cling-on while packing up my car.

Chad went upstairs and gathered his things. He decided to stay downtown since he already had a hotel reservation and tickets to the blues concert. When Chad was ready to leave, I showed him to the door. I thanked him for coming in to spend New Year's with me and gave him a big hug. He hugged me back and said, "I love you, Karen!"

I didn't know what to say, so I just said, "Oh, thank you. Text me when you get downtown to your hotel." Chad was not the guy for me, and it took spending four days with him to realize that. I felt a little bad I couldn't say the three words back to him, but I wasn't feeling it for Chad.

I told him that my feelings weren't moving in the right direction, and I didn't want to waste each other's time by prolonging the inevitable. I think I was just done with the relationship.

PART 6:

THE GOLF GUYS

CHAPTER 26:

FOUR WOMEN TOO MANY

My girlfriend Donna and I arrived at the golf course on the day of the outing and did the normal preliminary items in preparation for the day. When we arrived at the first hole, we met Sheila and Mary, the two ladies we were paired with for the day. We introduced ourselves and made all of the normal niceties. In the process of our introductions, we learned we had a person in common. Donna and I worked with Mary's son Dave.

I said, "What a small world it is!"

She looked at me and said, "Dave said he saw you and Chad on a boat last weekend at Shooters. He hardly recognized Chad!"

I chuckled and said, "Oh yes, Chad hardly recognized Dave either. It had been a long time since he saw him last." I acted like I knew what she was talking about and shrugged it off. I got into the golf cart with Donna and laughed.

She asked. "What is so funny?"

I told her what Dave's mom said to me about seeing Chad and me at Shooters the previous weekend.

Donna asked, "What was so funny about that?"

I said, "I wasn't at Shooters with Chad last weekend?"

I guess that would explain why Chad had been unavailable or unreachable for long periods of time. He seemed very distant and disconnected from me in the last couple of weeks. I was only seeing him one to two days a week versus the three to four when we started dating. Clearly, being exclusive meant something different to Chad than it did to me. I ignored what my intuition was trying to tell me.

This explained why Chad couldn't keep his country club tours straight! I felt like a fool for so many reasons! I questioned the fake behavior of his friends that knew and played it off. I felt an odd vibe at the outing from several of the women I had gotten to know over the last several months. Now I understand why!

Chad continued to date people while I committed to being in an "exclusive" relationship with him. I thought Chad was different, but I was wrong. He was a scumbag like so many men before him. Donna felt the brunt of my frustration for the next couple of hours and listened to me vent. We ran up his tab with drinks, snacks, and some pricy golf gear we got in the pro-shop.

We met Chad at a cocktail party for some drinks after the outing, and I pretended to be unaware of Chad's cheating ways. It wasn't easy because I was really pissed about the information I learned that day.

Chad's friend came over to our table and said, "Look at you, Chad! You are with two beautiful women! Are you sure you handle the two at the same time?"

My friend Donna piped up in her typical comeback style and said, "Based on what we learned today, I'm pretty sure he can handle four women at one time!"

It took all my might not to throw my drink in Chad's face and poke him in the eye.

The look on Chad's face was priceless. He went three shades of pale and was speechless. He knew he was busted but didn't know how bad. I must admit I enjoyed seeing him squirm in his own bullshit. I stayed until the end of the party, and Chad asked me to come back to his place for a glass of wine. His intent of having me over wasn't for any other purpose than to find out what I knew about his cheating. I declined his offer and went on my way. Our relationship was over, and he knew it. I never talked to Chad after that evening. He didn't call me, and I certainly didn't call him.

I later learned Chad was dating four women at one time, and I was one of them. He ended it with two women just prior to the outing. He narrowed down his selection to another woman and me. Only one woman remained after I dumped him that day. He married her four years later. To provide you some context to how we got here, I have to start at the beginning

After a six-month dating hiatus, I dove headfirst into the dating pool and became inundated by the masses of men who wanted to communicate with me. I typically like to take a step back and evaluate what transpired with the men I caught and released while on a hiatus.

I reflected on the things that went well and tried to understand the things that didn't. It's a period of time I like to focus on myself without worrying about looking at profiles or responding to messages. It's refreshing to clear my mind of the men I had met and the unsuccessful dates associated with them. Not worrying about all the minutia that comes with online dating frees up a lot of time and energy.

I was in a good place and decided it was time to try again. In no time flat, I was dating again. Let the swiping begin! I went on several dates over the next couple of weeks, and one by one, I eliminated the sketchy characters until I was down to one guy in particular. His name was Chad, and I was pretty sweet on him.

Chad was a handsome man about my age and was quite a gentleman. He was a golfer and also belonged to a country club. I was totally smitten by his courting skills, and he spoiled me like no one had in a very long time. He bought me a new golf outfit on one occasion and a new driver another time, as a couple of examples. I was not used to being spoiled and pampered in this manner.

On our third date, we went to his country club, and he gave me the grand tour, followed by dinner in the attached restaurant. He introduced me to several of his friends who were also there for dinner. Dinner at his club became a regular occurrence over the next couple of months, and I have to admit I really liked it. I could get used to this lifestyle.

We went to the club for our two-month dating anniversary, and Chad proceeded to give me the grand tour of the club *again*. I thought this was very strange. Did he forget he had already given me the "tour" two other times? It felt like I kept repeating the same date. We had a fabulous dinner at the club that night, followed by some hanky-panky at his house afterward.

After fooling around and sexually content, Chad put his arm around me and said, "We need to talk." *Oh boy!* When someone says those words to you, it can mean something good or bad, and I wasn't sure what to expect. He cleared his throat and said, "I want to be exclusive with you." I was relieved it wasn't something bad.

I replied, "I would love to be exclusive with you!" I hadn't been a one-man woman for a very long time but was excited to see where this relationship would go.

The intimacy between us was just adequate. It wasn't off the carts great but served the purpose of pleasure. The first time we fooled around, I noticed his *"thing"* was crooked. I had never seen such a thing and was perplexed by its shape. It resembled the letter "J" and was difficult to work with during sex. He could tell I was puzzled by his misshaped anatomy and offered up an explanation that his ex-girlfriend broke it during an argument. I never heard of such a thing but didn't want to call him a liar. When I voiced this bizarre condition to my best friend, she called bullshit. My one girlfriend told me it could be Peyronie's disease, which is fibrous scar tissue inside the penis that causes curved erections. I had never heard of this disease either, but it seemed legit. Chad said he was going to get it fixed, but that never happened when he was in my life.

I was sitting at work one afternoon when I got a call from Chad asking me if I was available that evening. I had no plans and was super excited to see him later that evening. Chad was always very punctual, and he picked me up promptly at 6 p.m. in a red party bus. The bus pulled into my driveway and out jumped Chad. I was excited to see him and curious to see what he had planned. There were four other couples on the bus and a cooler full of beverages. The bus took us to a variety of different bars for a Lakewood bar crawl, and the evening was a blast.

My next month or so filled itself with lots of golf outings, dinners, and parties. There was one particular outing to an Indian's game that left me with an unforgettable "Chad" memory. Chad's client gave him some incredible seats in the front row, along the first baseline. Chad had four tickets and invited my daughter and one of her girlfriends to join. I was never fortunate enough to have the opportunity to sit in such amazing seats before. We arrived at our seats wearing our awe-inspiring Indian's attire, but Chad wore white golf pants. *Who wears white pants to a baseball game?* I started to see a pattern with this pair of pants because he wore them on most of our dates.

We got situated and ordered some French fries, nachos, and hot dogs in addition to some drinks. The benefit of these ritzy seats meant you got a server assigned to you and could order food and beverages without ever leaving your seat.

Carols Santana came up to bat while we grazed on the grub we ordered while enjoying our incredible view of the game from these first-class seats. Santana connected with the first two pitches and fouled down the first baseline very close to our seats. Then came the third pitch and crack. The ball came right at us. The ball crashed into my daughter's cardboard food container and covered me from head to toe in ketchup. I had it in my hair, on my face, on my pants, and all over my game jersey. I didn't even get the foul ball because I was still processing what occurred.

Chad was flabbergasted by the incident that just happened. He was very concerned, and, most importantly, he wanted to make sure I was okay. Ketchup was splattered all over his white golf pants. This was a good reason why you shouldn't wear white pants to a baseball game. Chad took me to the team shop and bought me a new sweatshirt to wear in lieu of my ketchup-stained shirt. I changed in the restroom and cleaned the ketchup from my face and hair.

Chad asked me if I was interested in playing in a women's golf outing at his country club. I love golf, so of course, I was interested in playing. He told me to invite one of my friends, and he would take care of all the costs. He even said I could charge all of our food and drinks to his account. I invited my friend Donna to play in the outing, and she graciously accepted my offer. I looked forward to a fun and memorable day of golfing with Donna!

This was when I started listening to my intuition, which is my superpower. I knew something was up with Chad, and I ignored my intuition. Lesson learned!

CHAPTER 27:

OCD MAN

―――

It had been a long week of work presentations, long fancy dinners, and early mornings with my client in New Jersey. I was happy to be homeward bound and anxious to sleep in my own cozy bed. I got to the airport with time to spare. I found a cute wine bar close to my gate and ordered an overpriced cabernet. I enjoyed every sip until I had to head to my gate.

They called my boarding group, and I made my way down the aisle to my seat. I looked around and noticed a handsome gentleman sitting across the aisle from me. He made eye contact with me and then looked away. He had entrancing blue eyes, a cute face, reddish cheeks, well dressed, and thinning hair on top.

When the opportunity presented itself, I introduced myself to him. "Hello, my name is Karen," I said and shook his hand.

He replied, "Nice to meet you, Karen. My name is Chad. Is Cleveland home for you, or are you going there for work?"

I explained I was in Jersey for a work event, but Cleveland was home. We chatted the entire flight back to Cleveland, and I thoroughly enjoyed our conversation. I plotted my strategy to give him my business card, so we could meet up again in the near future.

The plane pulled up to the gate and prepared to deplane. I felt a tap on my shoulder, and Chad handed me his business card. I happily took it and presented him with mine in return. I said, "Let's get together for a drink sometime soon."

He smiled and said, "I would like that very much. I will be in contact with you." We smiled at each other, deplaned, and went our respective ways. He was very charming and quite the gentleman.

He sent me a text that evening and let me know what a pleasure it was meeting me. He wanted to meet for a drink the following week and inquired about my schedule.

We picked up right where we left off on the plane when we met the next week. I asked the million-dollar question, "Are you married?"

Chad clarified his divorce would be final in the near future, so technically, he was a married man. The "marital" detail broke one of my personal dating rules, and I didn't know how to feel. He was one of the most normal people I had met in a long time.

We tentatively scheduled our next date and ended the evening with a wonderful kiss goodnight. I looked forward to our next date but knew I had to come to terms with the fact he was not divorced.

We communicated a lot in the week leading into our date, and I felt comfortable with him. I learned he loved golf as much as I did, and we made plans to play golf together that weekend. Things progressed nicely with this man I met randomly on a plane.

Chad lived downtown in a contemporary-style row home, and it was quite lovely. The kitchen was absolutely spotless, and I mean there was not a single crumb or speck of dust on the counters! Everything was perfectly in its place, and his bedroom looked like a stark white hotel room. Everything was very clean and looked sterile in an elegant yet simple way. The bathrooms were Clorox clean, with brand new white towels. This was the first *red flag,* and it screamed OCD.

My ex-husband was a tad OCD, and it was difficult to live with someone like that. It was one of the many reasons that led to my divorce. I vowed never to allow myself or my children to live in that type of environment ever again. It made me extremely nervous Chad was such an OCD clean freak.

The first time we had sex, if you can call it that, Chad behaved strangely, to say the least. The foreplay was great, and I had no complaints with that part. Ten minutes later, he collapsed to his side, looked me directly in the eyes, and said, "That was simply amazing!"

What was amazing?

He was sweaty and out of breath like we just spent an hour making love, but we didn't! I fell asleep replaying the nonevent in my head! I headed home a little sexually dissatisfied, around 3 a.m.

Chad called me on my way home and was very chatty.

I said, "Why aren't you back in your warm bed sleeping by now?"

He said, "I am washing my bedding, so I will be up for a bit yet."

I asked, "Why are you washing your bedding at this hour of the night?"

He replied, "I didn't want to sleep in dirty linens from our 'fun' tonight."

I was still bewildered and had nothing to say. *Red flag!*

The next time I was at Chad's impeccably clean condo, I looked around and said, "If you think there will be no crumbs or mess with two children, you're kidding yourself." Chad said, "Are your kids messy?" Chad, and his soon-to-be-ex, never had children, so it was hard for him to understand how messy kids can be. The thought of entering into a relationship with an OCD partner again wasn't an option and was a deal breaker for me.

Chad and I parted ways shortly after that discussion because we came to an impasse on the "cleanliness" expectation of a household and children. I am by no means a slob, and I keep a very clean house, but I refused to subject myself or my children to that OCD setting again. Been there, done that!

My self-confidence was a little bruised after this breakup. I had big expectations for Chad and I and was sad it didn't work out. There are certain *red flags* I can tolerate and others I can't.

How many *red flags* is too many, and should we tolerate any *red flags*?

CHAPTER 28:

FMC

My friends enjoyed our annual "Golf Hooky Day," playing eighteen holes of golf. My friend's buddy, Chad, joined us at some point during our round. He was my age, very attractive, stood about 5'9," had a great sense of humor, was super friendly, and loved golf! What more could I want? We had a super fun day of golf, followed by beverages in the club house.

Chad walked me to my car and asked if I was interested in going out to dinner with him. I told him I would like that and graciously accepted his invitation! I gave him my number and was very excited to see him again. Chad sent me a text message the next day just to say hello. I was elated he had reached out so quickly. This was encouraging! We made arrangements to meet for dinner that weekend.

We had a really enjoyable first date full of wonderful conversation and laughs. I was encouraged by how well this date went. I was leery yet confident in what I was feeling for Chad. I had been down this road so many times before, I lost faith in the process. I didn't want to get my hopes up but tried to be optimistic.

The next month or so was really nice, and the relationship developed the way I had hoped. We went to dinner a couple of times a week and talked often. Chad made me feel special, and he started to grow on me. We hadn't been intimate, and he was open to waiting until I was ready. I was glad he wasn't obsessed with having sex like so many men were. Chad lived forty-five minutes away, and my daughter lived with me, so the opportunity for sex hadn't presented itself. I enjoyed spending time with him and didn't see any *red flags* at this point.

Chad invited me down to his place for dinner. I was a little nervous and didn't know what to expect. It was a long drive, and it felt like I was driving to Colorado. I don't know if I envisioned myself enjoying this drive to Chad's house in the future without dread. I arrived at his place, and he welcomed me with a hug, kiss, and a glass of wine, which took the edge of my anxious feelings. We sat in his kitchen and enjoyed some wine while he made me dinner.

The menu of the evening included a salad, filet mignon, grilled asparagus, and a baked potato. This romantic dinner was lovely, he prepared the food perfectly, and everything was absolutely delicious. After dinner, we cleaned up the kitchen and headed into the living room. We enjoyed some passionate kissing, heavy petting, and almost the "S" word! I put the sex brakes on since I knew my daughter would be home soon, and I had to get going. I told him I would take a raincheck on the hot and steamy things that could have happened on the couch. I felt bad pulling the plug on some hanky-panky, but I didn't want to rush into it and wanted our first time to be special. I told him, "I don't want our first intimate time to feel like a wham bam, thank you ma'am moment." He totally understood my position, and we made plans to spend the weekend together when my daughter was at her dad's.

The weekend arrived, and Chad picked me up to meet my friend Donna and her husband downtown for dinner. We had an amazing meal and headed to a music venue to watch some live music with several other couples. We enjoyed the music until we all realized how depressing her songs were. The song lyrics of the ten songs we heard all included the words "I'm sorry" and recalled the trauma of every breakup in her life. We ended up leaving the event early because we couldn't take it any longer.

Chad was clearly buzzed and was slurring his words. How many vodka tonics were too many? Ten? I wasn't opposed to Chad having a good time, but not if you are driving. I was frustrated Chad wasn't disciplined enough to know his limitation with alcohol and drank himself to oblivion the night of our first sleepover. I had seen this behavior before and found it very unattractive. I drove home, and he apologized the entire car ride home for being so drunk.

We got back to my house, and as anticipated, Chad was ready to pass out. I was agitated, to say the least, and he knew it. He asked me what was wrong.

I responded, "Are you kidding me? This is our first chance to spend the night together, and you are hammered! I don't want our first time to be sloppy and drunken!"

Chad defended himself and tried to convince me he wasn't that inebriated. I knew by the number of drinks he consumed he was most certainly drunk.

We got into bed, and there was little closeness or affection because I wasn't in the mood to fool around with drunk Chad. He knew I was annoyed and tried to cozy up with me. He kissed me affectionately and hoped he could change my mood, which it did. Kissing progressed to foreplay, and my arousal level surpassed the aggravation I felt. Things got heated, and we headed for the *"home run,"* or so I thought!

Chad's performance expectation was questionable, based on what I wasn't feeling between my legs, and out of nowhere, Chad screamed out, *"Fuck my cock!"* He shouted out those three words over and over again. We weren't at that point in our relationship that talking dirty was acceptable.

My eyes were wide open under my closed eyelids. "What the hell was going on?" I thought to myself. The most ironic part, Chad's member was totally lifeless and looked like an uninflated balloon. I almost busted out laughing but didn't want to ruin Chad's non-moment.

The dry humping continued for about five minutes, and just like that, Chad rolled off me, gasped for air, and passed out. If I wasn't present in the moment, I would have believed we had incredible sex, but we didn't. Ten minutes later, Chad was passed out and snoring. This certainly wasn't how I envisioned our first "sex" night to go.

This wasn't a deal breaker, but it didn't endear me to the relationship. I slept horribly due to Chad's unbearable snoring. The sound coming out of him was beyond annoying and resembled that of a snorting, drowning hog.

He woke up early and was bright and chipper. I was exhausted due to lack of sleep and felt like I had sand in my head. He reminisced about our evening and admitted he drank too much.

I said, "Ya think?" I wanted him to leave, so I could get some well-deserved sleep. I kissed him goodbye and sent him on his way home. I got back into my bed and pondered the events from last night. I couldn't unhear his "Fuck my cock" shrieks! This is embedded in my mind forever!

The next couple of weeks were very busy for me, and I didn't see Chad. It was by design! I did some soul searching during this time and realized Chad wasn't for me. It took four months of dating to contemplate having sex with Chad, and it didn't seem very special to him. I would have found a way to be intimate with him before four months if I was truly into him. This should have been my *red flag!*

Chad talked about the future and vacations together. He would say things like, "We should plan a trip to Florida," or "When we retire someday, we can golf all the time." He obviously had deeper feelings for me and saw a much brighter future for us than I did.

I told Chad I didn't see the relationship going anywhere, and my feeling weren't progressing in the right direction. I let Chad know I wouldn't be attending his friend's wedding with him. I decided to end the relationship, which caught Chad completely off guard.

CHAPTER 29:

A REAL NAIL-BITER

———

It had been a long, nonstop, crazy, busy workday, and I was hangry. I didn't put anything out for dinner, and I didn't feel like cooking either. I stopped at a local watering hole on my way home because I needed food fast, and I loved the chicken wings at this particular bar. I was in the mood for some delicious, greasy, garlic parmesan chicken wings.

I bellied up to the bar in my normal fashion and ordered a drink and some well-done wings. I like my wings extra crispy, and this establishment makes them perfectly. I was doing some "people watching" when I noticed a handsome guy across the bar who made eye contact with me at the same moment. We smiled at each other, and I looked away discretely. In the blink of an eye, he was standing next to me and introduced himself as Chad. He wasn't in great shape, but there was something about him I liked. His smile was contagious, and he made me feel warm and fuzzy when he looked into my eyes it. I am a sucker for a man in business attire, and he sported a classy suit and fashionable shoes.

Chad was my age, an attorney, an avid golfer, and conveniently lived two minutes from my house. I enjoyed talking to Chad because he was fun to talk to and knew how to carry a conversation. He was witty and funny but could discuss serious topics too, and I liked that. He didn't talk politics and was down to earth.

Chad explained I met him at Octoberfest, a year prior, unbeknownst to me. I had no recollection of this past encounter but left a lasting impression on him. Chad and I talked until my wings arrived, and he excused himself so I could eat my dinner. I told him I would circle back with him when I finished eating or before I left. He bought me a drink and went back to his group of friends.

I inhaled my wings and enjoyed every single bite. I went over to Chad's table to thank him for the drink after I paid my bill. We exchanged digits, and I told him I'd like to meet up with him for a drink sometime.

He responded quickly and said, "I am currently dating someone, but I will let you know if that situation changes."

I was fine with that and appreciated the transparency. The majority of men in this same situation would be dishonest about their dating status and lead you on by playing games. I was dating someone too, but not exclusively, so I was free to date whoever I wanted.

I received a text message from Chad a couple of weeks later, and he told me the relationship he had been in ended. He invited me to dinner, and I accepted his invitation. We met for a casual dinner the following week, and I enjoyed getting to know Chad better. He had one daughter and two sons and was divorced for several years. He belonged to a country club, where he golfed frequently, and I liked that! The date lasted a solid four hours, which is an indication of a great date.

When Chad wrapped his fingers around his glass to finish his last sip of wine, I cringed! I noticed Chad had no visible nails on his fingers. They were all gnawed down to the nub. I became fixated on how revolting his hands looked and couldn't think of anything else. I envisioned him chomping on his fingers like a squirrel eating nuts. We started spending a decent amount of time together, and the relationship progressed nicely. It was super convenient we lived so close to one another, so he could run home for his children if needed. We dated for several months and agreed to be "*exclusive*."

Our relationship evolved to the next level of intimacy, and I was happy about that. Intercourse with Chad didn't make me crawl the walls or send me to the moon, but he mastered the art of foreplay. There was definitely room for improvement, and I looked forward to practicing with him.

Chad was a really good golfer, and we golfed at his country club often. He was fun to golf with and wasn't the competitive guy who felt threatened by a woman who could outdrive him.

Chad always made sure there were plenty of adult beverages in the cart when we golfed. I enjoyed a couple of drinks during golf, but Chad went through drinks like I went through tees. We usually had dinner at the club following a round of golf, which included several more beverages for Chad. I started to see a drinking pattern developing each time we golfed. I wasn't alarmed at this point, but my eyes were wide open to the situation. *Red flag!*

I loved trying new restaurants, and so did Chad, but he was a "regular patron" at the establishments he frequented. Chad, being the single guy, had a designated night, and standing plans with each of his married friends on the nights we didn't go out. Every night meant a different friend at a different local watering hole. It was the "*married guy de jour,*" and he got hammered five days a week. This was another disturbing pattern I saw with his drinking. *Red flag!*

When Chad got home from his guy dates, he would be horny and want to come over. There was only one occasion I allowed Chad to stop over, and that was the last. Chad called and asked, "Do you want me to bring over some gas station hummus?" I wanted to see Chad, and I certainly couldn't turn down gas station hummus, so I allowed him to stop over. When he arrived, it was apparent he was drunk. He was slurring his words and acting sloppy. He struggled to look me in the eyes without experiencing long blinks.

Fortunately, or unfortunately, Chad picked up a loaded gyro for himself. He scarfed down his gyro in about two minutes, and I said, "Did you even chew it, or did you swallow it whole?"

Chad looked at me with a mouthful of gyro and said, "Ha, ha, ha, I think I chewed it!" I couldn't understand him because he had a mouth full of food.

Chad opened the hummus he brought for me during his drunken stupor and started inhaling it with a piece of pita. I asked, "Are you going to leave any of that hummus for me, or are you going to eat it all?"

He put the lid back on the hummus, let out a couple of loud, gross belches, and plopped himself on the couch next to me. This was very unattractive behavior, and I wasn't impressed. *Red flag!*

I wanted Chad to leave, but before I could tell him to go, he lunged over and planted a wet, open-mouthed gyro kiss on me. I didn't expect that at all, and his breath was utterly horrendous from the loaded gyro! I pushed back and gave him a disgusted look.

He responded with, "What?"

I said, "You do realize you just ate a stinky gyro and garlic hummus? Your breath is horrible!"

I proceeded to tell him I didn't appreciate his drunk, obnoxious behavior. I said, "I would like you to leave, and I'll talk to you tomorrow when you are sober."

He left with his tail between his legs and a big sad face. He apologized the next day for his behavior, but it was clear his drinking was controlling his life. This was a big *red flag* that kept appearing.

We went to dinner a couple of days later, and he apologized again and again for his drunk behavior from that night. I finally got to see the inside of his house when we stopped to pick something up. It was obvious Chad's drinking was hurting his life. He had a beautiful home that needed updating, but he neglected these tasks due to his drinking. He started painting all the bedrooms but never actually completed one. There was random furniture and bedding piled up in the hallway. His place looked run down and was "that" house on the block that everyone frowned on.

I like my men to be somewhat handy and productive. It tells me a lot about a person's character when they start projects but never finish them. Chad was too busy drinking with his buddies to commit to finishing any of the fifteen projects he had started in the last ten years. Drinking was a priority! *Red flag!*

The final straw that caused the breakup happened on a Sunday afternoon in the fall. There had been a three-week period Chad and I hadn't seen each other due to personal commitments. He knew what time I was due back that Sunday afternoon, and I assumed he wanted to see me.

We didn't have any definitive plans but was excited about the thought of seeing him. I called him to see if we had a game plan to see each other. Chad answered his phone, and I could tell from the background noise that he was watching football at a bar.

I said, "What are you doing?"

He told me he was at a bar like I presumed.

I was pissed and said, "Really? I haven't seen you in three weeks and wanted to get together today!"

He replied, "Come meet me and watch the game with us?" I could tell in his voice he was already buzzed.

I said, "Umm… No thanks, Chad, I am going to pass on that offer!" I hung up on him because I had to cool off!

This moment defined where I stood in Chad's life. I wasn't a priority. I was fourth in line behind his family, friends, and drinking.

I called him about an hour later to let him know how disappointed I was about his decision to make plans with his buddy versus me, considering we hadn't seen each other in three weeks. I explained I wasn't looking for someone who put drinking and partying at the bars every night as a priority over me.

Run in the other direction when your partner makes getting drunk every day a priority over everything else in their life.

CHAPTER 30:

CAPTAIN CRUNCH

———

I wish I could reclaim the worthless time wasted on Chad. My girlfriend raved about a new dating app, so I decided to give it a try for *one month*. One and done! I entered all the pertinent information, hit enter, and just like that, I was dating with my *"eyes wide shut"* in hopes of finding *my* special person. I had no idea the next six weeks would be my validation to write my book.

I perused through what felt like a million pictures of men. This drill wasn't new to me, and I felt defeated on the first day. I came across a picture of a guy I knew three years earlier. I sent him a message and asked, "Are you the guy I took golf lessons from three years ago?"

He replied quickly and said, "Yes, Karen, I am that person!"

I said, "I thought you were happily married?"

He added, "I am happily divorced after twenty-three years of marriage to a narcissist!"

I questioned how happily married he was back then, based on the derogatory, chauvinistic comments he made about his wife! I wasn't attracted to Chad three years ago because he was thick around the waist, lanky, thinning hair, and had braces. His current profile reflected a better version that was tall, in shape, bald, and no braces.

I was curious about his story and made plans to meet him for a drink and potentially some golf. We quickly caught up on my life, and then he gave me the long-winded, two-hour version of his story. His divorce was an emotional subject for him, based on his angst, and he had nothing but horrible things to say about his ex-wife. *Red flag!*

Golf was fun, and it was nice getting to know Chad on a different level outside of lessons. I was pleasantly surprised by my first date, despite the ex-wife rants.

I decided to never move forward with a guy riddled with divorce rage since my relationship with Chad.

I invited him to the dinner party I was throwing that weekend, and he accepted my invitation. Chad lived fifty miles away and was concerned about drinking and driving home after the dinner party. Did he not have the discipline to stop drinking or stay sober enough to drive? I offered him my guest room as an option but made it very clear nothing sexual would happen! He understood and was happy to have the option to stay if necessary.

The dinner party ended up being a lot of fun, and my friend and her husband left promptly at 8 p.m. We relaxed with a beverage and started watching a movie.

I was tired and wanted to go to bed. I told Chad he could sleep with me but reiterated that there would be no hanky-panky. He obliged, and we just cuddled.

I woke up at 4 a.m., and Chad wasn't there. I found him asleep, on the couch, in my family room. I asked why he was there?

He said, "I couldn't sleep because your dog kept growling every time I moved!"

I explained, "She won't bite. She growls so you don't roll over on her."

The next morning, he pointed to my dog and said, "*It* is the reason I didn't sleep well!" He called my ten-pound dog an "it!" *Red flag!* I told him, "My dog is an extension of my family, and if you want to be in my life, you have to like my dog."

I won't date someone who doesn't like my dog.

Chad was eager to see me by midweek and took me out for an impromptu dinner. I learned, during dinner, Chad loved Captain Crunch Cereal and ate it every morning for breakfast. *How old are we?* Chad laughed and said, "You'll need to get a box of Captain Crunch and some flavored half and half if you want me to stay over again!"

"*It's official. We're exclusive!*" he said. His declaration caught me off guard, but I was relatively happy with how things had started off, and I wanted to find out sooner than later if this thing with Chad was a bust.

My best friend played in the dating arena before finding her soulmate, so her opinion is invaluable to me, and I wanted to get her feedback on Chad. She has a good read of people and is usually spot on. I made plans with my bestie and her fiancé that weekend.

Chad and I went on an eighteen-mile bike ride the afternoon prior to our dinner plans that evening and had a very enjoyable time.

We made all the normal introductions at the restaurant, but the conversation at the table was very odd and uncomfortable. Chad refused to participate in any dialogue other than golf or politics and even became argumentative when he got called him out on some questionable things he said. It felt extremely awkward, and I could tell by the disapproval on my girlfriend's face she didn't care for Chad's attitude.

We said our goodbyes after dinner, and Chad and I headed back to my house. I was embarrassed by Chad's pompous demeanor at dinner and dreaded the anticipated feedback from my friend.

It had been a long time since I was close with a man, and I thoroughly enjoyed the adult activities during our first intimate night together. He came equipped with his own personal lubricant, which I thought was odd.

Chad didn't like that my ten-pound dog sat on the floor watching us and grumbled, "It messes with my concentration and interferes with my ability to perform!"

My tiny dog messes with your concentration? Now that's funny! I understand not having my pup on the bed during adult activities, but my dog jumps off the bed on her own and returns when the fun is over.

I woke up to find Chad missing again and assumed he was on the couch. My dog slept by my feet when he was over, not to disturb his sensitive mental state. I heard him making coffee at 5 a.m. but continued to sleep because I wasn't his entertainment. I made breakfast, and then Chad headed home.

My girlfriend called me the next day and gave me the low down on Chad. They weren't impressed at all and thought his behavior was strange. She gave him the benefit of the doubt and thought he could have been nervous. She told me not to throw in the towel quite yet.

I invited Chad to participate in my fun, noncompetitive annual golf outing but said, "If you decide to play, you can't be competitive."

He accepted and said, "I don't know how to have fun. I was always taught to win."

The golf outing was enjoyable, but Chad became very annoying at times because he couldn't leave the "golf-pro" character at the door and have fun. He took the whole day way too seriously and was out to *win*! *Red flag!*

Chad invited me, my son, and his girlfriend for a fun evening on his pontoon boat. I figured Chad and my son would get along since they both collected guns. However, Chad was adamant he didn't want to talk guns that night. My son knew more about guns than he did, and Chad didn't want to appear less knowledgeable. I saw a pattern developing here, and I didn't like it! It was a very nice evening on the boat overall, despite Chad's over-the-top paranoia when my son smoked a cigar.

The four of us went to dinner for sushi after the pontoon boat. I asked my son for his opinion of Chad a couple of days later, and he said, "He seemed okay, but he was really freaked out about my cigar. I also didn't like how he thinks COVID-19 is part of life's natural selection process." In code, that meant my son wasn't a fan, but he could tolerate him if I liked him.

Next up was the *island weekend* at my friend's house on Marblehead, with my daughter Nikki and her boyfriend Nate. The weather forecast was going to be perfect. The three of us took the early ferry, so we could get to the house and get settled, and Chad took a later ferry.

The four of us started playing a frisbee game called "Bottle Bash" once we got back to the house. This was the first time I had ever played this game, and it was fun. The game consists of two poles, two beer bottles, and a frisbee. A beer bottle is placed on the top of each pole and positioned approximately twenty to thirty feet apart. The purpose of the game is to toss the frisbee and attempt to knock the beer bottle off the pole. Points are awarded accordingly.

The fun ended when Chad became extremely competitive and forceful with his turns. Chad looked at me and said, "You suck at this game!" I gave him a death stare, and he knew I was pissed, but he didn't care. He sucked the enjoyment out of the game because he was a sore loser. *Red flag!*

The mood changed when he started to poke insulting jabs at Nikki. He tossed a super-fast throw at her and said, "Have fun catching that one, girlie!" It hit her hand so hard she got a bruise and broke her fingernail off. His intent was to hit her and not the bottle.

I scolded him and said, "That is enough! No one appreciates your aggressive behavior. This is just a game!" He shrugged it off and didn't care. *Red flag!* We called it quits on the game and walked into the house with Nikki and Nate.

I will never tolerate a man who is malicious and disrespectful to my children.

My friend Tom took us for a ride around the island on his boat and dropped us off at an adjacent island, where the four of us indulged lobster bisque soup at the Boardwalk. In addition to the lobster bisque, I ordered a lobster roll, and Chad got a salmon sandwich. It wasn't cheap, but I let Chad pay since he arrived at the island empty-handed. It had been a whole ten minutes when Chad suddenly stood up and said, "That's it, this sandwich is taking way too long." I reminded him they said it would be ten to fifteen minutes to prepare his sandwich. He got up, stormed over to the counter, and demanded his money back.

We headed back to our homebase island on the little shuttle boat called the "Sunny S." I had enough cash to cover Nikki, Nate, and myself, but Chad would have to cough up money for his ticket. We relaxed for a while once we got back to the house.

We took Chad's car and headed to one of the three bars on the island. We ordered some drinks, and Chad got some food since he didn't eat earlier at the Boardwalk. I was still stuffed from lunch and only ordered a couple of drinks. Chad paid for his food and drink, and I was left to cover the remaining tab.

We got back to the house, and Chad really wanted me to retire to the bedroom to fool around, but I stayed up until the wee hours talking and drinking with everyone in the house. I wasn't in the mood for Chad, especially after the behavior he exhibited throughout the day.

The four of us headed to the dock in the morning to go jet skiing. My daughter and I went out first, and Chad and Nate waited on the rock beach, or so we thought. We came back about forty minutes and found Nate sitting there alone. We inquired about Chad's whereabouts, and Nate said, "One minute he was sitting on that rock over there, and the next minute he was gone!"

Chad's car was still there, so he couldn't be too far. I couldn't call him because my phone and clothes were in his locked car. Nate called back to the house to see if he was there, and he was not. Nate said, "Well, we lost Chad!"

We started to walk back to the house when we saw Chad. We asked him where he was, and he said, "I was down there checking out the shitty par-three golf course if you can call it that! I also stopped to talk to some dude about his boat."

I said, "Next time, it would be nice if you let someone know where you are going."

He looked at me like "F*k you," got into his car, and we went back to the house.

We played cornhole after dinner, and once again, Chad became overly competitive. I was just astonished by Chad's horrific conduct.

We went to the island pizza place for dinner our last night. We had some drinks, pizza, and good conversation. The server was confused when we asked her to split the check various ways. I told the server to give me the check.

My friend said, "Are you sure?"

Chad looked at her and said, "We got this!" He didn't contribute a dime to the bill, which meant "*I got it.*" We ordered some drinks at the bar after dinner, and once again, "Mr. Cheapskate" didn't pay at all. What a jerk!

The next morning Chad was up early and ready to go. He left around 7:30 a.m. for the 8:15 ferry, which is a tad early, seeing as though the ferry dock is only five minutes from the house. I was glad he left, so I could relax and enjoy my remaining time there. This weekend was a real eye-opener.

I will never let a person take advantage of my kindness and generosity.

I went down to Chad's place the following week. I needed to address his behavior at the island and knew the evening might get awkward. I entered his place and saw him sitting on the couch checking out the new "Bottle Bash" game. I said, "How funny you decided to get that game."

He said, "I loved that game." There was a lot of awkward silence, and he knew something was up.

We went to dinner, and I discussed his unattractive competitive side from the weekend. I reviewed all his fucked-up behavior from the past couple of weeks, and he didn't have an explanation for it except, "I was raised to always win and never lose! I don't know how to just have fun!"

I let him know I would not tolerate that bullshit behavior and explained how it made me feel, especially how he treated my daughter. I got a bunch of lip service from him and never got an apology, but he actually paid for dinner.

We were headed to Chicago a couple of weekends later, and I really wanted to uninvite him after the island weekend, but my "tarot card" girlfriend told me I would learn a lot from the trip, and it was important he go with me. I made it very clear to Chad he was accompanying me on the trip as a copilot and not for the purpose of "meeting my parents."

We arrived at my sister's house and got settled in. We played golf a couple of times that weekend with my nephews, which I enjoyed. My nephew had made the tee times for us and paid in advance. I made sure Chad paid him, so my nephew didn't get stuck picking up the cost for everyone's golf. Chad paid my nephew for his portion of the golf costs only!

The golf rounds started off great until competitive Chad showed up, and Chad's game fell apart. "*The wheels came off*" and Chad's attitude became worse, and he was clearly agitated with the world.

I gave Chad a tour of my hometown, and I could tell he was impressed. We stopped at my parents when the tour was over and visited with them. My sister showed up unexpectedly, and we decided to get sushi for lunch on our way back to my sister's.

We stopped and got sushi as planned and had an enjoyable lunch with my sister. I grabbed the check and paid before my sister knew what happened. She looked at me and said, "Are you sure?"

Chad looked at me and replied, "She's got it!"

I figured he would put his card down and split the cost with me, but no such luck. I couldn't believe it. What a piece of shit!

That night I woke up at 3 a.m., and Chad was missing. I figured he had gotten up and found another place to sleep like he had done so many times at my house. When I did make it downstairs in the morning, I found him curled up in a ball on a couch in my sister's living room. Weird!

I had a wonderful visit with my family and was sad when it was time to leave. We were packed and ready to head out by 9 a.m. The drive took the normal time, and Chad took over the music during the ride once again and only played songs he liked.

He didn't offer to pay for gas, tolls, my sister's lunch tab, or my golf. He was treated to the wonderful meals at my sister's home and thought he would have offered to pay for something. *Red flags* were popping up everywhere with this guy. The Karen snowball was rolling downhill at full speed. *If someone is a cheapskate, I will run and not look back!*

I told Chad I had a happy hour in my neighbor's driveway upon arriving back home, and I gave him the option to go or head home. He decided to stay and slammed back two vodka drinks in about ten minutes. I said, "Wow, that's a lot of booze fast!" He just snickered at me, grabbed the folding chairs, and headed out the garage door to the happy hour next door.

I introduced Chad to my neighbors but could tell he made people feel uneasy. He mumbled things under his breath, and I wished he had gone home. Finally, he couldn't stand being there any longer and excused himself. He went back to my house, gathered his things, and left. I was relieved and started to enjoy the happy hour. I knew my relationship with Chad was over, and I couldn't wait to end it.

Chad sensed something was wrong over the next couple of days. He asked, "Is something wrong? You have been very distant."

I explained, "In the six weeks we have dated, you haven't brought me a single flower, card, or made a single gesture to make me feel special." I clarified that I had paid for virtually everything between the island weekend and Chicago, and he contributed nothing.

He said, "Are you calling me cheap?"

I said no, "I am calling you a freeloading mooch!"

He sent me a text an hour later that read, "This isn't going to work, is it?"

I replied, "It doesn't appear it will."

He called me immediately to discuss our situation further. I unleashed on him for the next thirty minutes and vented everything that had bothered me from the day we met.

When I was done, he simply said, "It isn't going to work when the person you're dating calls out all your imperfections while dropping the 'F' bomb. All the best!"

I said good luck and hung up on him. Just like that, I was single again, and I was ecstatic.

PART 7:

THE RHINESTONE COWBOYS

CHAPTER 31:

MR. IOWA

———

Online dating was still in its infancy stages and had just started to gain traction in the social media arena. Facebook was also relatively new and was the platform to be on. I gave the Facebook thing a try too and created a profile for myself. It wasn't long before I established a sizable group of friends associated with my profile. I liked the concept of reconnecting with people from my past. Facebook kept me up to date on the lives of friends and privy to upcoming events. It seemed I was accepting new friend requests or friending people on a regular basis.

Several months after launching my Facebook profile, I got a friend request from Chad, who was someone I knew from high school. He went to the private high school versus public, but I knew him from parties on the beach back in the day. I accepted his friend request, and in no time, we started to chat and catch up on life. He was in the middle of a very messy divorce, and that was a topic we commiserated about. We chatted regularly and rekindled the friendship we started back in high school.

Chad was tall and handsome. He was very outgoing and had a super fun personality. We got along great and seemed to click. We made plans to meet up over the holidays when we were back in our hometown. Chad tore his Achilles tendon four weeks before we met, and I thought this would put a kibosh on our plans for sure, but the plan stood firm. The plan was to have dinner in downtown Chicago and stay overnight. I love Chicago and welcome any opportunity to stay in the city.

Chad was picking me up at my parents' house, and I anxiously awaited his arrival for our long-awaited rendezvous. When he pulled into the driveway, I got a big smile on my face and felt "*happy*" butterflies in my stomach. I can count on one hand the number of times a guy made me feel all giddy. Chad crutched his way to the door, where I greeted him and introduced him to my parents. I got into his car, and we started on our way downtown.

We were only about ten minutes away from my parents when Chad suggested we stop for a beverage in Highwood. I couldn't help but wonder if he was having second thoughts about going downtown with me. I guess this would be a great chance to make sure there was truly a connection between us before committing to the entire night together. I can count on one hand the number of times I spent the night with a man on the first encounter. We ordered drinks and fell into some very comfortable conversations. It felt like we had been dating for years, plus Chad was hilarious and made me laugh! I love a guy who can make me laugh and smile.

We found ourselves staring deep into each other's eyes. I leaned in and kissed him on the lips, and he reciprocated with several more wonderfully soft kisses. I felt like we had not skipped a beat since high school. Chad paid the tab, and we headed back to the car and continued on our way to the city. We passed the test!

We checked into the hotel and got settled into our room. We headed out to start our date in the city. We meandered around and took turns picking spots to stop and have a drink. Ironically, many of my favorite places turned out to be his favorite as well. I felt like we had so much in common, and this was a very uncommon situation for me to experience. We ended up at Shaw's Crab House for dinner, where we gorged on oysters, crab claws, and crab legs. I was so incredibly full by the end of the meal I wanted to unbutton my pants. Not really, but I was very, very full.

We headed to Hugo's Frog bar after dinner, which is a very trendy upscale bar/restaurant. It was Chad's childhood friend Lee's birthday, so he met up with us for a couple of drinks to celebrate. I didn't know Lee at all during high school, but he certainly seemed nice enough.

Lee's family owned a large, nationally renowned company. We conversed and enjoyed our drinks when out of nowhere, Hannah appeared. I've known Hannah since grade school but didn't realize she was such close childhood friends with Lee and Chad.

Hannah's family owned a nationally renowned business publication, and she wanted for nothing, and I mean nothing. We all sat around and talked, and Hannah ordered a bunch of appetizers for us to indulge on. When it was time for us to head out, Hannah flashed her America Express Sapphire card and picked up the entire tab. I wasn't going to fight her for the check, and I didn't feel guilty about it because her monthly allowance from her parents was $10,000. That is not a typo! It must be nice!

Chad and I went on our way, but we stopped for a night-cap on our way back to the hotel and reminisced about Lee and Hannah. Chad smiled and said, "The last time the three of us were together was twenty-something years ago. We were inseparable back then."

There was lots of kissy face and ogling going on between Chad and me. I was super turned on and looked directly into Chad's eyes and said, "Let's go back to the hotel and have sex!" Chad looked and me with a sheepish grin and said, "Hell yes!" We sucked down our drinks in record time and practically sprinted back to the hotel. I was horny, excited, anxious, and nervous all at the same time.

The door to our hotel room closed behind us, and things got hot and heavy. We managed to make our way around the bed, despite the cast on his leg. Emotions were intense, and so were the hours of hot, sweaty, amazing sex. The next morning, we were so exhausted that we slept until an hour before checkout and had to rush out of the hotel.

I was pretty hungover, and all I wanted was some greasy McDonald's to help ease the nausea I was experiencing. Chad took the back roads back in search of a Happy Meal for me. How is it when you want McDonald's there isn't one to be found? We were only fifteen minutes from my parents when we finally found one. I ordered a Coke, two cheeseburgers with extra onions, pickles, and a small fry. *It was the most delicious thing I had ever eaten!* We made our way back to my parents, where we kissed some more, we said our goodbyes, and agreed to talk later that day.

We continued to talk and chat a lot over the next several months, and we decided to meet again over Easter when I came back to town. We agreed to repeat our holiday excursion to this city. The relationship continued to grow, and I really liked him. *My heart knew it.* I hadn't felt this way for anyone in a very long time. The long-distance relationship progressed nicely and blossomed like an Easter Lily into something special.

Easter was upon us in no time, and we were headed back to the city. We had dinner at Shaw's Crab House, which had become our special place. We made our way to an upscale place called Tavern on Rush, where we enjoyed several more adult beverages.

We met up with Chad's friend Lee again, and he informed us he and Hannah were dating. Chad's jaw hit the floor when he heard this news.

Chad and I continued dating long-distance, and he religiously made the ten-hour drive from Iowa to see me at least once a month, and I always looked forward to his visits.

Chad got a call from Lee during one of his visits. Lee and Hannah were getting married. *Married?* Not only were they getting married, but they were getting hitched the following week. We could hardly believe what we heard, especially Chad, who was in disbelief about the upcoming nuptials. Three months later, Chad learned Lee and Hannah were getting divorced. *Divorced?* Chad and I looked at each other said, "WTF!" Chad looked relieved by this development.

Chad surprised me with a trip to Key West, and I was elated. Key West was a very romantic place to be, especially with someone I was falling in love with. I hadn't said "I love you" to anyone since my nine-year relationship but was definitely falling for Chad. I take those three words very seriously and wouldn't just throw those words out without meaning them wholeheartedly. My heart was headed in that direction but wasn't ready to say it. We did all of the typical Key West bar crawls and also made our way to several of the renowned restaurants. Time flew by, and we found ourselves headed back home in the blink of an eye. Chad headed back to Iowa and I to Ohio. We made some wonderful memories and looked forward to our next visit together.

Chad came out a month later for my annual Halloween party and also to celebrate my birthday. Chad took me to dinner for my birthday, and we had an enjoyable evening together. The next night was the Halloween party and he rocked his costume to a tee. His one task during the party was to make sure to watch the garbage and change the bag when it got full. He failed to do his one task and didn't contribute to the party cleanup at all. This was a turning point in the relationship for me. *Red flag!*

Chad was oblivious to everything around him but himself. I was really pissed and let him know just how disappointed I was when we crawled into bed. He wanted to fool around, and I turned him down. I was actually relieved when he headed back to Iowa the next morning. *Or so I thought!*

The next day was my birthday, and my daughter and I had plans to go to dinner. I had just gotten home from work when the doorbell rang. I answered the door, and Chad was standing there in a stylish suit, holding a bouquet of flowers. "Surprise," he said with a sheepish grin. I was completely caught off guard by this surprise development.

Little did I know, my daughter schemed with Chad behind the scenes to plan this secret surprise. We headed downtown to the Blue Point for dinner, which happened to be one of my favorite restaurants. We arrived at the restaurant, and I learned there were even more surprises. Five of my closest friends had been invited to dinner too and were there waiting for me to arrive. We had a wonderful evening, and I felt blessed to be surrounded by all these special people on my birthday. Chad left the next day and headed home for real this time. I didn't realize it at that moment, but that would be Chad's last visit to see me.

Several months passed, and the long-distance part of our relationship began to wear on me. I found myself doing some soul searching to get some clarity surrounding our relationship and its viability. Chad's kids were ten years younger than mine, and he was stuck in Iowa until his kids were at least eighteen, which was many years down the road. Moving to Iowa wasn't an option, and I came to the realization it would be ten years before Chad and I had the opportunity to experience a normal relationship together. This thought was very daunting to me.

It was with a heavy heart, and after a great deal of thought, I decided to end my relationship with Chad. I knew he wouldn't be happy about my decision but knew it was necessary. I called Chad and started the conversation with, "*We need to talk.*"

He said, "Uh-oh."

I explained my feelings about the distance between us and how I longed to be in a relationship with someone I got to see weekly. Seeing Chad once a month just wasn't cutting it for me anymore, and that justified the breakup in my mind. I explained it would be ten years before we had the kind of relationship I desired. I let Chad know I cared deeply for him and was only ending the relationship because our situation was geographically undesirable for me. If we lived in normal proximity to each other, I truly believed we would have gotten married and lived happily ever after. Unfortunately, that was not the case for us, and we parted ways. I hoped to remain friends with him, but regrettably, Chad didn't take the same position and was very salty about the breakup.

It wasn't a month later when I saw a bunch of pictures of Chad and Hannah surface on Facebook, and they looked very cozy. I couldn't help but wonder what was going on with these two. The rumor on the street suggested Chad and Hannah were an item and were living together. *Living together!* Less than two months later, I found out that Chad and Hannah got married and were living in the $4 million house purchased by her parents. *Married!* I saw some of the posted wedding pictures, and I couldn't believe it. They got married in Key West, which made me sad because I consider that our special place.

Six months later, I learned Chad and Hannah were getting divorced. *Divorced?* I knew it wasn't going to last, but I didn't think it would end that quickly. It wasn't a year later, and Hannah was married again, to another person.

It took a long time for Chad and me to become friends again, but we still keep in touch today and are friends. Chad still believes we will end up together one day. That remains to be seen.

CHAPTER 32:

THE DIDDLER

My third attempt at online dating played out like it had so many times prior, and I questioned my motivation to enter the dating arena. Likes and messages inundated me from different types of men. There were lots of swipes left and a few to the right.

I came across a man whose amazing smile caught my attention. His name was Chad, and he was very attractive and had a captivating profile! He was one of five guys I swiped right on. We appeared to have a lot in common, including golf. I messaged him with my typical line, "So tell me about yourself?"

He responded with a litany of tidbits, and we continued to exchange texts. I felt good about this guy and was ready to initiate a happy hour date with him.

I welcomed a weekend with no plans after a crazy couple of weeks. I committed to a relaxing Saturday night watching movies in my jammies. I just settled in on the couch with a glass of wine and a comfy blanket when my phone dinged. I looked to find a message from Chad. He wanted to meet for a spontaneous drink... *that evening*. His invitation tore me because I looked forward to my tranquil evening at home. If

I accepted his offer, I would have to shower and get all beautified. I went back and forth in my mind for about fifteen minutes before I decided to meet Chad for an impromptu drink. I jumped up off the couch and started my "get ready" process. I headed out about forty-five minutes later and was excited to meet Chad. I made my way to the agreed meeting location. He was even cuter in person than he was in his profile pictures. He had charming brown eyes, stood 5'8," in good shape, balding on the top, with a "hair horseshoe" around the sides.

We hit it off immediately and felt an attraction between us. We had drinks followed by dinner, and four hours felt like five minutes. I was on cloud nine and was happy I had decided to meet him. He walked me to my car and gave me an amazing kiss. He looked into my eyes and said, "I had a marvelous time tonight and want to see you again soon!"

I said, "I would love that." We made plans for our second date before ending our first. *This was a great sign of things to come…. or so I thought.*

We had our second date the following weekend, and I was anxious to see Chad again. I met Chad at a little wine bar, which offered great wine choices and an array of small plate food options.

I had a wonderful time, and Chad's food choices were delicious. Two great dates in a row? This was unheard of in the scope of my dating adventures. Chad put his arms around me at the end of the evening and said, "Do you want to come back to my place? I live like five minutes from here." I could count on less than one hand the number of times I had gone back to a guy's place on a second date. I was really torn between my own personal dating rules and what "*horny Karen*" wanted. I broke my rules and decided to follow him back to his place. I hoped my decision wouldn't turn into a Lifetime TV movie for me!

We were in Chad's condo ten minutes later. The condo was very spacious and open. There was a bunch of mismatched furniture and weird odds and ends. His place screamed divorced, single dad! Chad must have seen the perplexed look on my face and said, "This place is only temporary. I had to get it when I got divorced. My ex got all of the good furniture, and she gave me all this old shit!"

There was a camping tent set up in the dining room area. There was a twin bed inside and some loose clothes on the floor. I pointed to the tent and said, "What's with that?"

He said, "That is where my ten-year-old son sleeps! There are only two bedrooms, and he wanted his own space with privacy. He loves it!" I just let that one go.

We made our way into his bedroom, where things got heated fast. Chad was a great kisser, and I enjoyed making out with him. Things progressed, and I enjoyed every single second of our shenanigans. It had been a long time since I partook in such enjoyable adult fun. Most guys are good at one thing during sex, and everything else lacked. Chad nailed everything, including me! I glanced over at Chad's naked body before doing the deed and was pleasantly surprised by what I saw. The next thirty minutes redeemed my faith in having good sex. I had no complaints and left with a huge smile on my face. I was actually proud of myself for having such a wonderful time.

The weeks progressed, and everything was going great, for the most part. Chad had some strange eating habits. I began to notice the first tiny *red flags* on the horizon. Chad and I typically ordered individual entrées when we went out to dinner. When our food would arrive, Chad tasted a bit of his meal and critiqued it. He would then reach his fork across the table and taste my meal. This wouldn't have been an issue if he just took a taste, but he would almost devour my entire meal and then polish off his meal. On one particular occasion, I looked at him and said, "Are you going to eat all of my dinner, or are you going to leave some for me?" I was puzzled by this behavior. *I don't mind sharing my entrée, but really!* This ritual of Chad's played out again and again and became very bothersome.

Chad started to spend the night on a regular basis, and things felt very comfortable with us. Chad worked in Houston Monday through Friday most weeks. The airport was only fifteen minutes from my house, so he typically stayed over on Sundays to save time on Monday when he would fly out to Houston for the week. I didn't mind his absence during the week because it allowed me to have social time with my friends. I made myself available to Chad on the weekends when he didn't have his kids.

One morning while we laid in bed together in the morning sipping our coffee, I saw Chad reach down and start caressing the crease between his thigh and pelvis. He wasn't playing with his privates. He just stroked the area with his middle finger. When he was an infant, he probably sucked his thumb and stroked this area to self-soothe himself. I felt like he had been doing this his entire life. I began to notice this peculiar habit happened on a regular basis. I called it diddling. One morning I became so irritated by his diddling I said, "What the hell are you always doing there?" and pointed to the diddling area.

He replied, "It's a guy thing!"

I quickly responded, "That is not a guy thing! I have been with many men over the course of my life, and I have never seen anyone do that. It is definitely not a guy thing."

He had no comeback. I was able to compartmentalize it for the moment but knew it would continue to bother me. Then came the opportunity of a lifetime for me. Chad had to go to Italy for work and invited me to join him. I counted down the days!

The travel day finally came, and I was over the moon. I had never been on a long flight before. I typically don't sleep well when flying and rarely feel well-rested when I get to my destination. We kicked off our trip in the executive club with some free drinks and snacks. I figured having a couple of glasses of wine prior to our departure might help me sleep during the eight-hour flight—no such luck.

I ended up drinking several more glasses of wine and watching three movies during the flight. I was pretty buzzed and dozed off for only fifteen minutes. Chad slept like a little lamb the entire flight. I was exhausted and a little buzzed still when we arrived in Rome. I had bags under my eyes, and I felt disheveled.

We got our rental car and made our way to our swanky hotel in Rome. We checked in and got settled into one of the fanciest hotels I'd ever stayed. The next five days were incredible, and the trip was amazing. We toured Rome, Florence, Pisa, and some other small little towns along the way. We had several incredibly romantic dinners and made memories I will never forget. I could see a future with Chad and loved traveling with him.

The day before we headed home, Chad had a meeting with several of his colleagues. While they had their meeting, I meandered around the little shops in the quaint little town we were in. I found a cute little place where I ate lunch. I gorged on a delicious meats and cheeses plate, while I enjoyed a big glass of wine or two. Chad texted me right when I finished eating and told me to meet him at the restaurant around the corner, where his group was.

I joined them and had another glass of wine while they finished up. We stood up and got in line to pay the bill when Chad leaned back and started eating the leftover food off the plates at the table his team just left. It mortified me. I couldn't believe someone at Chad's management level would do such a thing. I gave him a look and said, "Did you just eat the chicken off Diane's plate?"

He chuckled and said, "Her and I have an agreement about food, so let's just leave it at that." I left it at that but continued to see this eating bullshit over and over. This was just another *red flag*.

I noticed a change in Chad over the course of the next three months. He was more distant and disengaged. I would hear his phone beep in the middle of the night, indicating he received a text message. I was so frustrated in the final month we were together. One of *our* weekends turned into him running his kids all around to their events. I know he was doing the dad thing, and that was great, but our time was limited as it was, and I became protective of my time with him. What irritated me was he purposely offered to do the driving for his ex. She wasn't out of town or unavailable to take the kids. He volunteered outright!

Two weeks later was our weekend again, and I hoped we would have a nice weekend together. I questioned our plans for the weekend when he called me on his way home from Houston. He rambled off a list of things he had to do once he landed back in Cleveland. Not one of those things on his list included seeing me. I didn't say anything and waited to see what developed over the weekend. I never heard from him again after that weekend.

It was awkward when Chad reached out six months later and wanted to meet. We ordered drinks, appetizers, and caught up on life. I never got the closure I wanted from that weird night six months prior. He walked me to my car, lunged forward, and started making out with me. I was caught off guard but liked his kisses. We met up four more times over the next six months, and it played out the same. Drinks, appetizers, and a make-out session.

It wasn't until the fifth time we met I understood what was going on. We talked about life and caught up like we had done over the last six months. Since we weren't dating, I started talking about some of the crazy dating stories I had experienced. I asked him if he was dating anyone, and he proceeded to tell me he had been dating someone for the last year. *What!* He reconnected with someone from his college days and spent a lot of time in Toledo, where she lived. I did the math in my head, and it made me question all those times we met, not to mention making out? I was perplexed but not totally surprised.

I had to wonder if the new woman in his life was the one who sent him the text messages in the middle of the night back when he stayed at my house. She was likely the reason for the distance I felt between us. It all made sense to me in an odd way. We never spoke again after that evening. I later found out he got married to the lady from Toledo.

I really thought I would marry Chad at one point, but in hindsight, I felt like I dodged a bullet. If he cheated on me when we dated, then he might have done it later down the road had we gotten serious. I moved on and jumped back in the dating pool again after Chad and I ended. I think of him from time to time but was grateful he gave me the opportunity to go to Italy for free. He came into my life for a reason!

CHAPTER 33:

YAYA GUY

Chad looked at me and said, "I have to talk to you about something important."

I said, "Oh boy!" *What could this be?*

He proceeded to inform me he was married!

I said, "What? Are you kidding me? Why are you just telling me this now?"

I knew he was too good to be true.

My mood went from rhapsodic, to confused, disillusioned, and irritated. Chad saw the change in my demeanor and said, "Please give me a chance to explain myself to set the record straight."

Chad explained how they lived separate lives while residing in the same house and planned to stay "married" for the sake of their children until they went off to college.

One of his sons was headed off to college that fall, and the other was a couple of years behind. The notion was to stay together until the boys left for college and then get divorced. Supposedly this marital situation was common knowledge with his sons, and they accepted their parent's living arrangements.

Chad lived in the finished basement, and the upstairs was his wife's turf. He defended there had been no intimacy between them for at least five years. They both went about their own lives and did their own thing. I really didn't know what to think of this whole situation, but he seemed very truthful and honest about it. I didn't feel like he was being deceptive with me.

I tried hard to understand the circumstances surrounding his situation but struggled to see the silver lining. Dating a married man totally broke my dating code.

"No dating married men, separated men, or men divorced less than a year."

Dating a man divorced less than a year is usually not a good thing. There is typically a great deal of residual angst, and I don't like getting caught up in that drama. I don't want to be the rebound person either because that is a recipe for a broken heart. It's just my luck. I met this amazing man, who gives me the "yayas," and he's frickin married.

I didn't want this revelation to be a wet blanket on our perfectly romantic evening, so I put the topic on the back burner for the moment. Despite the details that had come to light, we exchanged some sensual and spicy texts that evening, which made me blush. I liked this guy but was plagued by the reality that he wouldn't be available for five years minimum.

The next morning, I got a strange text from Chad. The text read, "If you get any text messages or calls from a Deb Jones, don't respond or answer. I will call you in a little bit to explain." His last name was Jones, so I assumed Deb was his wife? Why would she be contacting me? I was completely stumped and wondered what the hell was going on. I don't need a crazy man's ex in my life. Been there, done that, and wanted no part of that bullshit.

Chad called me several hours later and explained when he got home last night, he inadvertently left his cell phone on the kitchen counter. Unfortunately, his wife found his phone and snooped through the naughty messages we had exchanged over the last couple of weeks.

Chad and his wife lived separate lives, but how open was their arrangement? Were they allowed to date other people, or was that topic never broached between them? If Chad feared his wife would contact me, I assumed she wasn't happy to learn he was sexting with another woman. Chad told me, "If she contacts you, tell her you and I are just friends." This answered my looming question about their arrangement.

His wife never attempted to contact me, and it was quite a while before I heard from Chad again. I reached out to him on several occasions with no response. Maybe they decided to work it out after all. I was sad, hurt, and felt like the rug just got pulled out from under me!

I went from rainbows and unicorns to lonely and disenchanted.

I spotted Chad out with his family several months later, and he made eye contact with me. This was clearly an awkward position for him. Chad stopped by my table after his family left the restaurant.

"You look great," he said and gave me a quick hug. We had small talk for about ten minutes, and he headed out with his to-go order. Our waiter brought over a bottle of wine to our table and said, "Chad bought this for you."

Chad reached out to me a couple of days later and told me how great it was to see me again. We exchanged some texts about life, and I told him my fiftieth birthday was on the horizon. He asked if he could take me to dinner to celebrate. I reluctantly agreed but was excited to see him. We met at "our" neutral spot and drove in one car. He was sincerely happy to see me, as I was him. He reached over and handed me a fancy bag. He said, "Happy Birthday!" It was a gorgeous sterling silver necklace and bracelet. I loved it and put it on immediately.

We got downtown, and valet parked the car at an upscale hotel/restaurant, where we were having dinner that night. Chad arranged for a private table in a secluded corner. We talked about his "home" situation but didn't let the topic monopolize the conversation or evening.

Chad divulged the current state of affairs with his wife was extremely unpleasant. Chad disclosed his feelings for me to his wife, and it went over like a box of bricks. Though they lived completely separate lives, under one roof, their "dating rules" had never been established.

His wife threatened to ruin his relationship with his sons, his job, and his social standing if he continued to see me. That is why he backed off and went dark on me.

He held my hand the entire night and told me how much he loved spending time with me. We went up to the rooftop bar for a nightcap and some sweet, wonderful kisses. It was hard not to get carried away and jump each other right then and there.

He told me he was traveling to Columbus for a morning meeting. He jumped at the opportunity to stay the night when I invited him, and we quickly headed to my place.

We arrived at my house, and I opened a bottle of wine. We only had a couple of sips before things got spicy, and we headed into my bedroom, clothes flying everywhere. We fell onto the bed and were passionately fondling each other and getting busy. The unfortunate part was his inability to *"make it happen!"* In a blink of an eye, everything stopped. Needless to say, we didn't have a "little blue pill" to help us out, and this wasn't how I envisioned the night to go.

Chad looked at me and said, "I am sorry, I don't know what is happening. I want you so badly, but *'it'* isn't working." Chad felt horrible he wasn't able to perform. I tried to reassure him it wasn't an issue, and I was just happy to be with him. We talked for a little bit and ended up falling asleep holding each other.

A couple of hours later, I was awakened by Chad, and he was standing next to the bed, all dressed, with his bag in hand. He said, "I am headed to Columbus."

I said, "It's two o'clock in the morning? Why are you leaving now?"

He said, "I can't sleep and didn't want to disturb you."

I tried to convince him to stay, but his mind was made up. I got up and walked him to the door to say goodbye. A hug and a kiss later, he was gone.

I knew there were underlying reasons why he couldn't sleep. This was likely Chad's first time with another woman, other than his wife. He was faithful to his wife and had never been intimate with anyone else. Maybe at the moment, everything became real for Chad.

I never heard from Chad again after that night. I texted him many times over the years, with no response. It made me sad because I truly believe there was something magical between us.

Chad was one of the few people I've ever met that put me on cloud nine from the moment we met. My heart fluttered the first time ever I laid eyes on this man with thick, sandy blond hair, adorable dimples, and exquisite blue eyes that still resonate with me to this day. My connection with Chad was so incredibly natural and felt so comfortable. I felt like I knew him for years. This was a rare occurrence for me because only three people have ever made my heart blush the way Chad did. I really thought he was the one!

Every time I heard his marvelous voice or read his text, it made my heart race, and my hair follicles tingle. Chad made me feel special, treated me like his queen, and was generous to a fault. I wasn't accustomed to this treatment from my previous relationships, and he was everything I looked for in a partner, with the exception of his marital status. Every date felt like a fairy-tale and left an unforgettable memory in my mind.

His kisses were soft, gentle, and put me over the moon. When he kissed me, he would cup my face with his hands and French kiss me like he did it for a living. The sexual tension between us was "*red hot*" and aroused me to the point I wanted to ravage him right then and there. I waited a long time to meet an extraordinary man, who made my armpits sweat and gave my heart the "Yayas."

I felt such a bond with Chad I was willing to wait for his situation to change so our worlds could align the way I envisioned. I was heartbroken when our love story didn't play out how I had dreamed. I often wonder if Chad and his wife worked through their problems and stayed married or ended up divorced. Chad knew where to find me if he was interested, and I refused to chase someone who didn't want to be caught.

The moment I feel unwanted in a relationship, I simply stop trying. I don't look back and will walk away knowing they weren't my person!

PART 8:

CONCLUSION

CONCLUSION

I got myself into bed after hosting a successful dinner party for some friends when my boyfriend decided to pick a fight with me. I scolded him for starting an argument after we both had been drinking, but he decided to drive home anyway. I told him, "If you leave, we are done." Unbeknownst to me, he slipped on my front step and fell down.

We didn't communicate again until Sunday evening when I received a text saying, "Hospital, brain bleed, concussion, MRI...."

I responded, "What? You are at the hospital?"

He replied, "Not now. I am home now resting."

I asked if he needed anything or wanted me to come over, and he said no. A couple of hours later, I FaceTimed him, and he was completely lethargic and said the doctor had prescribed him Demerol after his MRI. *Red flag!* I told him to get some rest, and I would touch base with him in the morning.

I texted him several times over the next two days, and all his responses were illegible and wonky. On Wednesday, he called to let me know his friend was taking him to the hospital because he still had a bad headache.

I said, "Do you want me to meet you there, or can I come to take you?"

He replied, "No, I will update you later. I just want to make sure that everything is okay."

I asked him, "What hospital, and what friend is taking you, so I can stay updated on your situation?"

He told me what hospital and said, "I can't give you her cell number due to HIPPA laws." What? *Red flag!*

I sat there for a couple of minutes and thought if the situation was reversed, I would want him to be with me. I packed up my laptop and headed to the hospital. When I arrived, I texted him and said, "Have you been seen yet, or are you still in the waiting room?"

He responded, "I am in a room, getting pretests, and then off to X-ray."

I responded, "Okay, I just got to the hospital, so be looking for me."

He went radio silent, and I didn't hear anything from him for over an hour.

I went into the emergency room, went to the information desk, and asked about his status. I said, "My boyfriend is somewhere in a room getting prepped for an X-ray. Where can I find him?"

The woman spent several minutes trying to locate him, based on the information I provided. She looked at me and said, "He is not here! The last time he was here was two years ago."

What? I said, "You mean to tell me he wasn't here on Sunday?"

She said, "No, he was not."

I was beyond pissed off! I left and went to my car and took a very deep breath. I texted Chad and said, "I just went into the ER, and they have no record of you being here since 2019. I am going back home. I don't know what kind of game you are playing, but I want no part of it."

It was about an hour and a half later when he responded, "My $10,000 Rolex isn't working, and I've lost all track of time!"

I sat there pondering my next move and wondering what the future held for me. I recently ended a relationship with someone who I thought was my end chapter. What we had seemed so promising, and I saw a future with him, until I didn't. He had so many characteristics I look for in a partner, and I was so optimistic about where it was headed until it wasn't. He was the first person I trusted with my heart and "loved" in fifteen years. I have no regrets about my time with him and truly believe people come into our lives for a reason, a season, or a lifetime. In his case, it was a reason and a couple of seasons.

I am not ready to put myself out there again because I am still processing the events that led to the breakup. My heart needs to heal before I allow it to love again. I will definitely jump into the dating pond when I am at peace with how things ended and am in the right mindset to move forward.

I haven't given up on love and am confident I will find the man of my dreams.

I just haven't met him yet!

I hope all the lessons I have learned from my dating adventures and stories will guide me in the right direction, down the path I'm supposed to go. The thought of heading down that road again is quite daunting, to say the least, but I will stay the course and look for love in "all the right places," or at least, I hope!

There are "plenty of carp" in this dating cesspool, and it sucks we have to weed through them before finding our diamond in a dumpster. I often ask myself, "What would their mother's think?" Who raised these people to be such dating disasters? No sooner do we think we found a good one, and they show their true colors, and we have to kick them to the curb.

It's like seeing a valuable item from afar at a garage sale, but up close, it's just a worthless piece of shit. The struggle is real, but we have to create some shitty chapters in order to write our final chapter and appreciate the journey.

I know many of you have been in this exact place before and question the worth of allowing ourselves to be vulnerable. Why would we open our hearts to potentially be hurt or broken once again? We typically take the path of least resistance to avoid being dejected or disappointed.

I have so many shitty stories and a litany of unsuccessful attempts at finding love but refuse to throw in the towel and give up. There is someone out there who will fill my heart with the love I deserve and make it sing from the rooftops for everyone to hear. He will respect me like no other and will never make me question his love for me. There will be no lies or hidden agenda, and my heart will be at peace to enjoy every ounce of love he gives. My intuition will tell me I am in a good place instead of being on high alert. He will be faithful to a fault and never play head games or be deceitful. There won't be questionable things that don't add up and make me second guess my own sanity. Everything will fall into place, and our worlds will align in perfect harmony.

There is beauty in the struggle if we choose to open our minds and see it.

There will continue to be horrible dating stories and heartbreaks, but we need to rise above it. Each of these adventures are lessons we need to learn to lead us to our end chapter or happily ever after.

Stay the course, my friends, and hold your head up high. Our "happily ever after" is out there, and we need to be vigilant in our journey to find it. Everything happens for a reason, and sometimes we don't know the reason until after the fact, but it will all make perfect sense when it's supposed to.

I will keep on keeping on and continue to write more stories until I find my end chapter or my true "swipe right"!

ACKNOWLEDGMENTS

———

Dennis and Carol Herrmann, Kim DeBoer, Nicole Cacioppo, Chris Cacioppo, Meryl Stern, Kent Hamilton, Deb Machutas, Rachel Placentia, Kenneth Parker, Duncan Hogg, Brian Britt, Carmelina Suydam, Frank Cerney, Scott and Joan Herrmann, Donna Easdon, Catherine Herrmann, Al DuPont, Nick Kolb, Amanda Haws, Bob Boutin, Andrea Franzese O'Brien, Enrique Rodriguez, Stacey Herrmann, Melissa Sabo, Jeff Bailey, Rhonda Verb, Kip K. Coco, Shirley Lane, Rob Starre, Adrian Frederick, Gail Bindernagel, Mike Goldsberry, Noreen Hernan, Sharon Gentry, Mitchell Zimmer, James O'Connor, Mr.& Mrs. Pete Packard, Aimee Lawler, Denise Puening, Karen Zelina, Sandra Isvarin, Mary Lovell, Dan Boos, Kerri Hershey, Randy Lipp, Jamie Field, Patty Schattler, Jessie Hamed, Anca Kocian, Daniel Conlon, Cindy Marquardt, Jessica Henry, Robert Rawlins, Susan White, David Steckel, Pam Juris, Elisabeth Pederson, Kimberly Jovanov, Sandy Ammar, Vicki Salvaggi, Lyn Lucius, Erin Loschetter, Teri Albus, Renita Jefferson, Diedre Kearney , Greg Duhaime, Demi Faraday, Susan Mena, Johanna Ljubic, Debra Goetz, Mark McClaine, Paul Mayer , Mary Van Bergen, Kathy Hable, Tom Meyer, Sheree Laborie, Jennifer Winters, Karyn Carlin,

Kathleen Forgan, Maryanne Ozak, Meri Halupnik, Maria Nigh, Janine Downs, Julie Ann Deal, Rich Carle, Ron Maihofer, Becky Olson, Ramona E Bosak, Daniel Gawne, Vicki Bracanovic, Justine Lemanowicz, Karen Walsh, Jennifer Dambrosio-Cooper, Emily Lockshine, Rhonda Buynak, Jacqueline Helgert, Lynda Boldt, Mareena Gentry, Carol Abraham, Erin Frey, Kevin Whalen, Diane Ewanko, Stephanie Hammar, Jim Calaway, Tom Corner, Ken Laugel, Richard Harmon, Lysa Hynes, Susan Cox, Tim Richter, Polly ReQua, Jeanne Leone-Schmit, Heather LaBay, Joe and Donna Cipollone, Cammie Bartholomew, Rita Collins, Rachel Sheaters, Michelle Thur, Victor Adu-Gyamfi, Elsa Haggerty, MacKenzee Tilley, Gregg Langtry, Jaime Caraballo, Laura Schaefer, Kaity Scott, Melissa Waclawik, Biff McCabe, Monica Kraszewski, Stephanie Callahan, Belinda Webb, Scot Fenderbosch, Amy Elder, Cheryl Webster, Tim Fink, Michael McNamara, Christine Jacobsen, Nora Steele, Debbie Daugherty, Meghan Radel, Christine M. Colna, Jennifer Pollack, Kristin Ostrum, Dylan DeBoer, Colleen Dugarte, Diana Hausrath, Susan Jensen, Debbie Rikess, Darian Chen, Peggy Sura, Lisa Roberts, Sarah Dilts, Blair Putz, Lisa Bartosh, Beth O'Kain, Melanie Metzner, Sara Sadaghiani-O'Dell, Mary Mohr, Laura Page, Thomas Ungar, Susan Hackett, Trish Dougherty, Eileen O'Donnell, Marsha Eichinger, Gina LaPietra-Edidin, Perry Brown, Rachel Bushey, Megan Davis, Judy Benedict, Doleh Dawn, Holly Bennett, Robert DeHart, Victoria Van Cura, Kelly Damore, John Rzeczycki, Jennifer Began, Judi Cole, Autumn O'Neill, Richard Leskovec, Brian Allabastro, Joe Wagner, Mary Mosher, Sally Swarthout, Tracy Mack, Naomi Lovejoy, Tracey Brady, Eric Koester, Kathleen M. Nofel, Anna Guglielmo, Jim Kerver, Sharon Boggins, Miki Ferenczy, Bonnie Belda, Mel Price, Kathy D. Nofel, Beth Wood, Karen

Staztsko, Tracy Johnson, Sabina Becker, Jennifer Livi, Karen Gommel, Deann Mealey, Therese Brandt, Karrin Sherer, Stephanie Gripp, Cynthia Hebert, Kylie Schoppe, Sonia Domanko, Andrea Svoboda, Carol Miller, Joel F Salas, Steve Wilson, Kaitlyn LaFayette, Stacey Wessner, Jenny Grossenbacher, Hannah Kircher, Anthony Martin, Angee Mantell, Jesenia Medina, Sharon Posner, Vanessa Moehring, Sarah Longfield, Nicole Jansen, Laurie Wolohan, Judith Matsko, Carol Strachan, Jonathan Tan, Biagio Russo, Tracy Bartaway, Richard Hall, Christopher Popp, Barb Nitzsche, Lisa Kmichik, Jo Ann Szczotka, Nickolas Nejadfard, Sarah Simon, Angela Kaleal, Alison Dygert, Debbie Lee Glacken, Cassandra Venorsky, Lisa Wood, Kaitlin Piper, Stephanie Brackett, Diana Shulsky, Suzanne Hinsberg, and Mohammad Y Suleiman